Mind in Buddhist Psychology

Mind in Buddhist Psychology

Translated from Tibetan by

Herbert V. Guenther
University of Saskatchewan

Leslie S. Kawamura
University of Saskatchewan

DHARMA PUBLISHING

 TIBETAN TRANSLATION SERIES

Calm and Clear
The Legend of the Great Stupa
The Natural Freedom of Mind (forthcoming)

International Standard Book Number 0–913546–07–0; 0–913546–06–2 (pbk)
Library of Congress Catalog Card Number: 74–24373

Typeset in Fototronic Laurel and printed by
Dharma Press, Emeryville, California

Dedicated to all beings swept by the tide of conflicting emotions, that through a clear understanding of the workings of the mind, they may attain liberation.

Foreword

Ten years ago, Tibetan Buddhism and its psychology was not very well known in the West. But with the translation of texts such as this, the practical psychological teachings of Buddhism are now beginning to materialize.

The subject of this book is self-knowledge. That is, until we thoroughly examine the nature of our mind, we cannot really be aware of who we are or why we are here. Just as an intoxicated man, lost in his own mind-created distortions, is unable to judge or control his actions, without an awakening into true knowledge we can only continue to create problems for ourselves and others.

The complexities of our mental patterns and the turbulence of upsetting emotions join like earth and water to create a kind of mud which we call 'samsaric mind'. Until we can cleanse ourselves of inner confusion and penetrate the various 'layers' of this mind, our judgments and actions will only reflect our inherent restlessness, like bees trapped in a jar. We can see them moving around in certain patterns, but without understanding their situation they can only move in Samsaric realms—each with its own unique loss of freedom. On the other hand, by properly investigating our immediate situation, we can learn how an integrated patterning of mind can totally free us from our self-imposed restrictions.

The Abhidharma systematizes Buddha's teachings and is one of the best ways we have of knowing ourselves. As a science of mind, the Abhidharma is such a vast subject that one could spend a lifetime studying the tradition of just one school. This text in particular, through its analysis of the mind and its mental events, is a useful beginning.

A person without understanding is like someone with no tongue who is unable to distinguish the bitter from the sweet. Similarly, when the various 'tastes' of sensations, feelings, perceptions and cognitions become muddled, we lose our ability to discriminate true knowledge from opinions and mere speculation. Often we just accept anything that comes in the door and calls itself knowledge. But if this text is to be useful, it should be examined carefully and critically.

We wish to thank Dr. Guenther and Mr. Kawamura for working so diligently on this translation, and everyone at Dharma Press who helped to produce it. Through future efforts, we hope to publish much more material on the Abhidharma, such as Mi-pham's *mkhas–'jug,* so that the vast and practical psychology of Buddhism will be available to the West.

TARTHANG TULKU RINPOCHE

Head Lama of the Tibetan
Nyingma Meditation Center
and the Nyingma Institute
Berkeley, California

Contents

Description
of Illustrations

Frontispiece

Asaṅga and Vasubandhu, the two brothers, are seated together with Asaṅga's teacher, Maitreya, above. Asaṅga is depicted receiving knowledge by inspiration; Vasubandhu holds a sacred text, indicating his vast scholarship and knowledge of the Abhidharma. The text of Asaṅga, *mngon-pa kun-las btus-pa* (Abhidharmasamuccaya), is an abridgement of the first two chapters of his Yogācāryabhumi, which employs the Hīnayāna Abhidharma teachings in the Great Way of the Mahāyāna. Vasubandhu's great treatise, the *mngon-pa mdzod* (Abhidharmakoṣa) revived the Abhidharma teaching which had been lost in a fire at Vikramaśila monastery. Both brothers started out on their individual paths, but Vasubandhu was later much influenced by his older brother, Asaṅga.

Page xix

dPal-sprul O-rgyan 'Jigs-med 'chos kyi dbang-po, one of the most renowned Nyingma lamas of the nineteenth century, is shown here upon a teaching throne. He represents the refinement and return to basic principles of study and practice which characterized this dynamic period of synthesis and tolerance.

Page 2

Mañjuśri, the Bodhisattva of discriminating awareness, is the inspiration for true understanding. He holds the flaming sword of discrimination in his right hand and the book of knowledge in his left.

Page 17

Nāgārjuna, the famous dialectician and father of Mahāyāna philosophy, who lived around 150 A.D., is shown displaying the Dharmachakra mudra, symbolic of turning the Wheel of the Dharma. His *rin-chen 'phreng-ba* (Ratnamala) and *bshes-sbring* (Suhṛllekha), which are often quoted in this text, were letters of advice written to a king of this period.

Page 34

Śantideva, a great pandit of Nālanda University, brilliantly proclaimed the Bodhisattva ideal of Mahayana in his *spyod-'jug* (Bodhicaryāvatāra) and *bslab btus* (Śikṣāsamuccaya). His works have continued to be studied by all schools in Tibet since the tenth century.

Page 71

Āryadeva, the illustrious disciple of Nāgārjuna, is shown with a defeated opponent at his feet. A master of philosophy and science, his works include the Catuḥśataka.

Page 106

Tsong-kha-pa, the founder of the Gelugpa sect in Tibet, is depicted upon a lion, indicating that he is an incarnation of Mañjuśri. His *lam-rim chen-mo* has been used in Tibet for centuries as a basic text for providing a foundation in Buddhist scholarship.

Page 113

Lord Buddha, the Light of the World from whom all teachings originate, is shown upon the traditional teaching throne with symbols of the six perfections which in him have flowered.

Preface

'The Necklace of Clear Understanding: An Elucidation of the Working of Mind and Mental Events'[1] by Ye-shes rgyal-mtshan (1713–1793)[2] is an autocommentary on his own verse text[3] which explains the mind and its fifty-one mental events in 177 four-lined stanzas.

In the colophon to his 'Necklace', Ye-shes rgyal-mtshan states that he stayed at the bKra-shis bsam-gtan-gling monastery on the border of Nepal and Tibet, and that he was the disciple of Blo-bzang-bzang-po, of Blo-bzang-ye-shes-dpal-bzang-po (1663–1737), the second Panchen Lama, and of Blo-bzang-rnam-rgyal. That he belongs to the dGe-lugs-pa school is evident from his title [Yongs-dzin] and from the fact that he copiously quotes from Tsong-kha-pa's (1357–1419) works and standard Indian Yogācāra sources. In fact he builds his presentation around Asaṅga's *Abhidharmasamuccaya* (51 mental

---

[1] *Sems dang sems-byung gi tshul gsal-par ston-pa blo gsal mgul-rgyan.*

[2] A biography of the author has recently been published as Volume 11 of the *Gedan Sungrab Minyan Gyumphel Series* under the title, *Biography of Tshe-mchog-gling Yongs-'dzin Ye-shes rgyal-mtshan*, by 'Jam-dpal rgya-mtsho (1758–1804), the Eighth Dalai Lama.

[3] *Sems dang sems-byung gi tshul rnam-pa bshad-pa'i sdom tshig rin-po-che-i phreng-ba.*

events as against the *Abhidharmakoṣa*'s 46 mental events) and Tsong-kha-pa's *lam-rim chen-mo*. In his own words,

> I, Ye-shes rgyal-mtshan . . . composed this work . . . by making the *Abhidharmasamuccaya* the basis and by embellishing it with statements from Tsong-kha-pa and his disciples. . . . [Fol. 51]

In this way, he offers the reader what may be called the 'officially approved version of Buddhist ideas that have come from India'. On the other hand, for what can be done with these ideas practically, we have to look to other sources, above all the rNying-ma-pa tradition which we have utilized in the introduction and in our notes. Nevertheless, from Ye-shes rgyal-mtshan's account, we can learn that positive mental attitudes produce positive situations for man's growth, while negative ones have the opposite effect. Another important observation is that any emotion affects the whole mind. For example, in a state of anger which is a negative state, there cannot be present a positive state such as confidence or tension release. The only way to overcome negative states or events is to strengthen the positive ones. To give an example, when assiduousness and confidence are present, there is no room for arrogance or skepticism; while negative emotions merely reinforce negative attitudes, positive emotions lead to growth and health.[4]

The 'Necklace of Clear Understanding' belongs to that group of literature called Abhidharma which concentrates on the training of one's critical cognition by methods of proper inspection. The Abhidharma, in particular as codified in Vasubandhu's *Abhidharmakoṣa* and Asaṅga's *Abhidharmasamuccaya*, is a systematic approach to understanding the world as man's horizon of meaning. For example, the *Abhidharmakoṣa*

---

[4] For an account of these mental events in relation to the path and stages, one should look into other texts such as the *Pañcaskandha-bhāṣya* by Pṛthivībandhu (P. ed. 113, No. 5560).

begins with a broad analysis of the psycho-physical constituents, such as the *skandhas, dhātus,* and *āyatanas* (Chap. 1),
and then presents the mind and mental events that deal with
these topics (Chap. 2) and orders them into the various levels of
the mind's world (Chap. 3). This interpretation, as well as
construction, is assisted by man's actions (*karma*) (Chap. 4)
which are sustained by the emotions operating overtly or co-
vertly (Chap. 5). While all this may involve man in the world
and force him to live uncritically, the major task is to grow and,
figuratively speaking, rise above the world. It is here that the
discussion of the various paths and stages begins (Chap. 6).
These stages are intimately connected with the distinct forms
of awarenesses (Chap. 7) which are further developed and made
a firm basis for a meaningful existence of man in his world
through contemplative processes (Chap. 8). In all these processes, the mind plays a decisive role.

We wish to acknowledge and express our gratitude to
Tarthang Tulku, Head Lama of the Tibetan Nyingma Meditation Center and the Nyingma Institute in Berkeley, for his avid
interest in our work and for his encouragement which spurred
us on; to Mr. Leonard van der Kuijp for proofreading the text;
and to Dharma Publishing and Dharma Press for undertaking
the publication.

Introduction

The title of this book poses two related questions: Is it justifiable to speak of Buddhist psychology? and, if so, What is the nature of mind in such a framework? The first question can be answered easily in the affirmative since, in many respects, Buddhist ideas are close to contemporary currents in Western psychology which have moved far away from earlier postulational suppositions. Secondly, throughout its history, Buddhism has emphasized experiential knowledge rather than dogmas as the starting point of man's growth and has been less concerned with systems of concepts and sets of postulates which remain hypotheses to be tested. Consequently, Buddhist psychological methods of observation are concerned with a study of human potentialities as they now exist, as well as how to develop them in the future.

The Way

'The Way' [lam] is a short term for the fact that man controls his future because of his ability to perceive, to know, and to order what he perceives and knows. This ability is dynamically active at this and every other moment, for the mind cannot be a static entity or a mere state or function of consciousness. Rather, it involves questions of When? Where? Under what conditions? From which perspectives? and hence, the mind is an on-going process in a person's life history.

In other words, the central problem of Buddhist psychology is that of *personality*, which is understood as implying that man has to be true to his inner nature in whichever way it may be defined—after, and not before, integrative techniques have been applied. Such a conception has immediate bearings on the individual's responsibilities which are inextricably tied up with the dimension of 'seriousness of living' as contrasted with the shallowness and superficiality of behavioristic oversimplifications and silly reductions.

The 'way', as understood in Buddhism, is a continual unfolding of man's potential and passes through several stages or phases, each of them involving different references and different self-images. The 'way' begins with the 'accumulation' of all that is necessary for man's intellectual and spiritual growth [tshogs-lam], and then merges into the 'linkage' of what has been learned with further growth [sbyor-lam] which, as it were, results in a new vision or fresh perspective, enabling the beholder to see more easily the intrinsic nature of the universe and of himself [mthong-lam].[1] But this vision has to be kept alive. This is effected by the subsequent phase [sgom-lam], which is a 'live experience', and climaxes in the 'no-more-learning' phase [mi-slob-lam]. At this point, the individual cannot but perceive the world around him as-it-is intrinsically, as well as perceive all that constitutes this world as being harmoniously interrelated. Contemplative understanding is never a thoughtless and senseless absorption in an imaginary absolute, but is always active in the special sense of not interfering. Man's actions and

---

[1] On this gradation which involves a general understanding [go], a feeling-experience [rnyong], and a realizing understanding [rtogs], see 'Jigmed gling-pa's *sGom-phyogs dri-lan* in the *Ngagyur Nyingmai Sungrab Series*, Vol. 37, p. 97.

his very life become more meaningful once this phase has become operative. Furthermore, the 'way' involves the whole personality which is as much body as it is feelings, the mind, and man's set of values and interpretations. The Buddhist 'way' is thus most comprehensive in being a growth and health psychology.

The Accumulation Phase

The complexity of the Buddhist 'way' may be illustrated by the analysis of the phase of 'accumulation' by dPal-sprul O-rgyan 'Jigs-med chos-kyi dbang-po (b. 1808):[2]

> The accumulation phase is dealt with under five headings: (I) basis, (II) essence, (III) subdivisions, (IV) meaning of the word, and (V) levels.
>
> (I) The basis consists of (A) the body and (B) the mind. (A) The body refers to any living being in the realms of sensuousness and aesthetic forms, and (B) the mind refers to single-mindedness in the world of sensuousness and to the states of consciousness on the six levels of meditative concentration.
>
> (II) The essence comprises seven topics for self-growth: (A) to observe manners and morals individually on the level of an ordinary person; (B) to control the senses; (C) to be moderate in eating and drinking; (D) not to sleep during the first part and the latter part of the night, but to exert oneself spiritually; (E) to delight in being consciously alert and aware [of what is acceptable and of what is to be shunned]; (F) to cultivate those positive factors which are the cause [for one's real freedom, such as never to feel sorry for a positive action or attitude, to be cheerful, to be confident, to be devoted]; (G) and to generate diligence in listening to instructions, in thinking about them and in making them a living experience.

---

[2] *Lam lnga rim bgred tshul dangs bcu'i yon-tan thob 'tshul bye brag tu bshad pa*, in Ngagyur Nyingmai Sungrab Series, Vol. 41, pp. 238–244.

(III) There are three subdivisions: (A) a low-level accumulation in view of the fact that it is uncertain whether the 'linkage phase' will set in; (B) a medium-level accumulation in view of the fact that the 'linkage phase' will set in during a future life-situation; and (C) a high-level accumulation in view of the fact that the 'linkage phase' will set in during this very life. The first of these involves the four essential inspections; the second, the four proper exertions; and the third, the travelling of the path by means of the four foot-like supports of spiritual growth.

(A) The practice of the 'four essential inspections' is the 'way' that deals analytically with particular existents and has five topics: (a) the object inspected; (b) the manner in which it is inspected; (c) the essential factors of inspection; (d) the necessity of inspection; and (e) the meaning of the word.

(a) The object inspected is the body, the feelings, the mind, and the constitutive elements of reality. The body is a 'without' [in the sense of being the sensory apparatus making up the 'body' of a sentient being and the objects for this apparatus]; a 'within' [as one's own sensory apparatus]; and both a 'without' and a 'within' [as the sensory apparatus of others as well as of one's self].

Feelings are pleasant, unpleasant, and neutral.

Mind is an eightfold or sixfold pattern [most important is the concept-channeled perception].

The constitutive entities of reality are the motivational forces with the exception of feeling; the fourteen schemata of interpretation; and the three absolutes.

Unregenerate persons fancy the body as the basis of a self; feelings as the foundation of what the self enjoys; mind as the substance of the self; and the constitutive elements of reality as the foundation of the refinement of the self. [Ordinary people entertain the wrong notion that the emotions project (a person) into evil forms of existence, while refinement leads to liberation.]

(b) The manner in which the object is inspected is twofold: (i) general and (ii) specific.

(i) The general characteristics are impermanence, frustration-painfulness, nothingness, and nonexistence of an ontologi-

cal principle. These (qualifications apply to every object of inspection and hence) range from the investigation of the body to that of the constitutive entities of reality.

Here, the body is perceived as a decaying corpse, crawling with maggots, having this nature and this actuality, and not passing beyond this state of affairs.

All feelings are painfully frustrating. [Inasmuch as feelings are such as not to like unpleasantness but crave for pleasurableness, they are ultimately frustrating and hence co-extensive and identical with frustration. However much one tries to leave frustration behind, only to that extent there is pleasurableness. Because of its former unpleasant character everything that is felt is painfully frustrating.]

The mind is impermanent because it becomes something else due to the difference in its objects and its basis. [The objects and the senses are the basis. The cognition that operates through the senses changes from moment to moment].

All the entities of reality have no ontological principle. [In this context the personalistic principle is meant.]

The intrinsic characteristics such as the elementary forces of solidity and so on, as well as that which has the defining characteristic derivative from (the primary elementary forces) such as the eyes and so on, make up the body; experiencing is feeling; cognition of objects is mind; keeping the intrinsic characteristics apart is (what is meant by) 'constitutive entity of reality'.

(ii) The specific manner in which the object is inspected has to do with the difference in the objective reference (or the epistemological object), which for a follower of the Hīnayāna is his own body exclusively, while for a follower of the Mahāyāna, it is his own body as well as that of others; and with the difference in thinking about its observable qualities, which for a follower of the Hīnayāna is the notion of impurity, while for a follower of the Mahāyāna, it is the conviction that all that is is the open dimension of Being (manifest in being); and with the difference in attainment, which for a follower of the Hīnayāna consists in a sense of renunciation, while for a follower of the Mahāyāna it is the realization of a non-localizable Nirvāṇa, as there is nothing to be rejected or to be accepted once the real nature (of reality) has been understood.

(c) The essential factors of inspection are discriminative appreciation and inspection.

(d) The necessity of inspection is to resort to the antidote of becoming involved in the four perverse notions that come through sloppy thinking [The antidote is, in general, (the awareness that) the six kinds of sentient beings depend (for their existence) on *karma*, that *karma* depends on the emotions, that these depend on the four perverse notions that come from sloppy thinking, that these depend on the mind-as-such which is (an) ultimate reality and a radiant light. Mind-as-such does not depend on anything else. An analogy for this is the dependence of the elementary forces on space.]; and it is also the reason for making a start with the Four Truths. As is stated in the *Madhyāntavibhāga*, IV, 1:

Because of ineptitude, because of hankering as causality,
Because of foundation, and because of non-delusion,
The four essential inspections are to be undertaken
In order to make a start with the Four Truths.

(e) The meaning of the word 'inspection' implies that the follower of the Hīnayāna applies his discriminative acumen to the object of inspection, while the follower of the Mahāyāna applies inspection to the object of his discriminative appreciation. [Having distinguished between the general and intrinsic characteristics of the body and other topics by way of discriminative appreciation and then preserving its continuity by way of inspection is to apply inspection to the object of discriminative appreciation. To investigate by discriminative appreciation the epistemological object that is kept steadily before the mind by inspection, and then to become convinced that it has no ontological principle, is to apply discriminative acumen to the object of inspection.]

(B) The practice of the 'four proper exertions' is the 'way' that has come into existence through efforts. It has five topics: (a) the object (of one's exertions); (b) the manner in which one exerts oneself; (c) the essential factor in exertion; (d) the necessity of exertion; and (e) the meaning of the word.

(a) The object of one's exertions is fourfold insofar as refinement by positive forces or defilement by negative forces have come or have not come into play.

(b) The manner in which one exerts oneself is to generate an earnest desire for not generating negative forces that have not yet come into play [earnest desire precedes actual efforts]; to make efforts [which is to intend a state of tranquility, to broaden one's horizon, and to intend a state of equanimity]; to initiate assiduity [which counteracts states of depression and of ebullience]; to seize the mind [ie. to cheer the mind up by thinking of the (Buddha's) appearance if one should be in a state of depression]; and to settle the mind [ie. to draw the mind inward by feeling disgusted with Saṃsāra if one should be in a state of ebullience].

(c) The essential factor in exertion is assiduity.

(d) The necessity of exertion is to weaken negative forces and to strengthen positive ones.

(e) The meaning of the word 'exertion' is to sum up the abolition of negative forces. Or, it means to firmly settle the actions that are performed by the three gates of body, speech, and mind.

(C) The practice of the 'four supports of spiritual growth' is the 'way' of thoroughly effecting spiritual integration. It has five topics: (a) object; (b) the manner of growth; (c) the essence; (d) the necessity; and (e) the meaning of the word.

(a) Spiritual growth is concerned with the positive way.

(b) The manner of growth involves the abolition of five obstacles by resorting to eight endeavors. When one is about to exert oneself spiritually, laziness is the primary obstacle. To counter it, one has to resort to earnest desire and assiduity [standing in a cause-effect relationship] as well as to confidence [as a basis] and cultivation (of one's abilities) [which rests on confidence]. When one actually goes about exerting oneself, forgetting the instructions (and injunctions) is the primary obstacle. To counter it one has to resort to inspection which will not let the observable qualities of the objective reference slip (from one's mind). When the potential is brought to life, states of depression and of ebullience are the primary obstacle. To counter them, one has to resort to an alert awareness. The method of countermanding states of depression and ebullience involves keeping the mind steady as an antidote to not making use of what counters them, and practicing equanimity as a countermeasure to overdoing things.

(c) In general the essence of the 'way' is spiritual integration, and in particular it is spiritual growth which involves the abolition of all that is negative through concentrative efforts whose support are earnest desire, assiduity, intentionality, and critical assessment. [To become involved with what one is going to bring to life, because one trusts in it, is earnest desire; to go about it joyfully is assiduity; to become single-minded is concentrative integration; and to examine whether states of depression or ebullience vitiate (this state) is critical assessment.]

(d) The necessity of spiritual growth is the realization of all that comes from the desire to actualize spiritual growth and what it involves.

(e) 'Spiritual growth' is all the qualities and virtues such as the five 'higher' kinds of immediate awareness,[3] and since this serves as the 'basis' or 'support' for this realization, one speaks of 'supports of spiritual growth'.

(IV) The term 'accumulation' is used because it assembles the causes for absolute enlightenment.

(V) Level here means 'level of confidence' because of the active presence of confidence in the Real as absolute.

According to this account, 'spiritual integration' [ting-nge-'dzin] is the indispensable precondition for man realizing his own nature. What man really is is both what the individual already is as a mind-body unit and what he makes of himself. This is a resultant of a dialectic between growth-aiding forces and growth-inhibiting forces. This dialectic operates in the area of 'spiritual integration' and can be illustrated graphically on the basis of Mi-pham's *gSang-'grel phyogs-bcu'i mun-sel-gyi spyi-don 'od-gsal snying-po* (fol. 58bf) [See Appendix, Figure 1, p. 118].

---

[3] The five 'higher' kinds of awareness [mngon-shes lnga] are those possessed by ordinary beings. The five are: miraculous power; hearing human and divine voices near and far; knowing others' thoughts; the recollection of former lives; and the vision of beings passing away and then reincarnating.

Mind and Mental Events

It will be helpful for understanding the nature and place of 'mind' in Buddhist psychology to first clarify the symbolism involved. Theorems like 'mind' and 'mental events' seem innocent enough as common-sense terms, but in philosophical and psychological literature they are not used with their common-sense meanings; rather, they are given highly technical philosophical-psychological and contextual connotative meanings. A presentation of any subject matter is a body of propositions which itself is a set of concepts. A concept is a term to which a meaning has been assigned either by having it denotatively associated with some datum or set of data immediately present, or by having a meaning proposed for it theoretically by the postulates of a specific, deductively formulated theory. The former procedure leads to 'concepts by intuition', the latter to 'concepts by postulation'.

Thus, in traditional Western philosophy and (theoretical) psychology, 'mind' has been a postulate or, to be more precise, a syntactically designated universal, regardless of whether it was conceived (1) as the self or subject which perceives, remembers, imagines, feels, reasons, wills, etc., and which is functionally related to an individual bodily organism, or (2) as a metaphysical substance which pervades all individual minds and is contrasted with material substance. Underlying the first proposition is, of course, the postulate of a center 'which stands in a common asymmetrical relation to all the mental events which would be said to be states of a certain mind',[4] and which in its commonest form involves a Pure Ego which is different from the events it holds together. The postulational character of the second proposition needs no further elaboration.

---

[4] C. D. Broad, *The Mind and its Place in Nature*, p. 558.

In Buddhist psychology 'mind' and 'mental events' are concepts by intuition whose complete meaning is given by something immediately apprehendable, and as such they are denotatively given particulars. This is evident from Ye-shes rgyal-mtshan's account. He says,

> To be aware of the mere facticity and haecceity of an object is mind [sems], and on the basis of this objective reference to become involved with the object by way of other specific functions is said to be the operation of mental events [sems-byung]. [Fol. 4a]

He then continues,

> To be concerned only with the objective reference but not with what the other specific functions perform, is mind [sems] as a primary operation, while an awareness which becomes involved with this object by way of these specific functions, such as those following the operation that deals with the objective reference, is a mental event [sems-byung]. [Fol. 4b]

There are several remarks of a general logical nature to be made.

(i) We may begin with the number of terms to which a given term may stand in the relation 'R'. If A is the progenitor of B, there may be many terms other than B to which A stands in the same relation. In the case of 'mind' and 'mental events' we have both a many-one and a one-many relation. The former says: the relation 'R' is such that when the referent is given, the relatum is determined, but there may be many referents: sems-byung R sems. The second is the converse of the former: sems R sems-byung.

(ii) If a number of terms [sems-byung] stand in a common relation to a certain other term [sems], it necessarily follows that they stand in a symmetrical relation to each other. If 'feeling tone' [tshor-ba], 'conceptualization' [du-shes] and so on be children of 'mind', they stand in the relation of 'brother-or-sister' to each other.

(iii) It is tempting to see in 'mind' a center, a certain particular existent or kind of Pure Ego which stands in a common asymmetrical relation to all the 'mental events' which would be said to be states of a certain mind, or, since 'mind' is itself an event, to see it as being of the same nature as the events which it holds together. Buddhist psychology, however, has generally rejected the assumption of a center in either sense. In any case, if a number of terms [sems, sems-byung] be interrelated in a characteristic way, it follows that there is something to which they all stand in a common asymmetrical relation, even if there be no center in the system. The reason is that each of them is a constituent in the fact that they are all related to each other in this particular manner. It is this *fact* that stands in a common asymmetrical relation to all other terms.

The rNying-ma-pa philosophers must be given credit for having noted this implication and for having clearly distinguished between 'mind' [sems] and 'mind-as-such' [sems-nyid]—between *pure fact*, of which, strictly speaking, we can say nothing, although we may use words to denote it so as to find in the immediacy of our experience (before it is channeled through words and concepts by postulation) what the words mean, and *described fact*, which by its nature is such that we have formed a concept of something and now attribute the characteristics of which we have the concept to pure fact which cannot be conceptualized. But in conceptualizing a pure fact, we have already falsified it and, in so doing, are forced to go further and further and farther and farther astray.

Following the technical diction of Buddhism, the distinction between 'pure fact' and 'described fact'—the one being, in terms of cognition, 'pure awareness or cognition' [rig-pa], the other, the 'lack of pure awareness' [ma-rig-pa]—presupposes pure awareness [rig-pa], but 'described fact' does not presuppose 'pure fact'. Hence, if 'mind' [sems], as distinguished from 'Mind-as-such' [sems-nyid], is equated with 'lack of pure awareness' [ma-rig-pa], as contrasted with 'pure awareness' [rig-pa], certain consequences follow. 'Lack of pure awareness' is listed among the 'basic emotions', and yet it is co-extensive with 'mind' with which the 'intellectual' functions are associated.

This shows that the distinction we ordinarily make between 'emotions' and 'reason' is a bifurcating description leading away from 'pure fact'. What we so describe by 'mind and the emotions' constitutes a malfunction of 'Mind-as-such' or 'pure awareness' or, to use a more comprehensive term, 'psychic energy'. (Again it has to be emphasized that these latter terms are pointers, symbolic ways of referring to an experience, but not symbols for some thing or other.) But even in this malfunctioning, the 'original psychic energy' (psychic energy here is understood as the positively 'good', or man's inner nature which, if it is allowed to guide his life, will let him grow in health and happiness) is not totally obliterated, but is present as 'appreciative discrimination' [shes-rab]. Appreciative discrimination is a value cognition, not an arbitrary evaluation, and contrasts sharply with the 'demands' [yid-la-byed-pa] that are constantly made by the ego, itself a demand or fiction [yid-la-byed-pa], on what is. These demands are inextricably intertwined with the powerful emotions of passion-lust and hatred-aversion (Khrid-yig, 54).

The contrast beween 'appreciative discrimination' and 'ego-centered demands' thus highlights the conflict between two major opposing forces in each of us. Through making demands we attempt to impose on and to interfere with all and everything; above all, we tend to cut ourselves off from the possibility of seeing ourselves as unique and whole human beings and, as a consequence, we merely proceed under the aegis of suitability-for-purpose, of making everything no more than a means to our selfish, if not paranoid, ends. While through 'appreciative discrimination', we would be able to discover the potential for growth and health that is in us and to develop it so that we might, and could, grow more and more into a human being.

It is for this reason that the 'positive mental events', as aids to growth, play such a prominent role in the analysis of 'mind'. A 'good' or 'real' human being is one in whom all the human capacities are fully developed and functioning well. It seems that man as a living being demonstrates in his very nature this urgency for becoming more fully human, which the Buddhists indicated by the technical term de-bzhin-gshegs-pa'i snying-po, which can be paraphrased as 'man's quintessence being the pressure towards Buddhahood'. Klong-chen rab-'byams-pa succinctly states in his *Chos-dbyings rin-po-che'i mdzod* (129a),

> When intrinsic awareness [rig-pa] has been divested of minding [sems] and of the mistaken appearances that go with minding, there is no other way but to go to pure and unadulterated Buddhahood, because man's very nature, which is Buddhahood, has been laid bare in view of the fact that it has been divested of the obscuring forces.[5]

The obscuring forces are precisely what is otherwise termed 'mind' [sems] which we can now more accurately define as a malfunctioning and which therefore is placed at the beginning of the Twelvefold Chain of Dependent Origination,[6] marking

---

[5] A similar idea is found in 'Jig-med gling-pa's *rNam-mkhyen-shing-rta*, an autocommentary on his *Yon-tan-rin-po-che'i-mdzod* (p. 792), where he quotes the Uttaratantra, II, 3, in support of this.

[6] Twelvefold Chain of Dependent Origination, see Mi-pham's *mkhas-'jug*, fol. 17b–23a; *Ārya Śālistamba Sūtra*, edited by N. Aiyaswami Sastri, the Adyar Library Series, No. 76, Adyar Library, 1950; and, Steven D. Goodman, 'Situational Patterning: Pratītyasamutpāda', in *Crystal Mirror*, Vol. 3, Dharma Publishing, 1974, pp. 93–101.

the growing involvement in growth-inhibiting forces that have us 'groping in the dark', 'running around in circles', in brief, erring and roaming about in Saṃsāra. This situation itself is to be considered as an incentive to do something about it, which means that first of all we have to find out what has 'landed us in this mess' and, as an aid to finding out, we have the analysis of 'mind' and 'mental events'.

The Necklace of Clear Understanding

An Elucidation of
the Workings of Mind and
Mental Events

Verses of Veneration
and Intention

I bow with folded hands to him who is inseparable from
Lord Mañjughoṣa,[1] the reverend and excellent teacher.
And I pray that he may accept me in his love for all times.

I bow to the supreme protector, Śakyamuni,
Who illumines the world where he looks
By his Omniscience from which all obscuring darkness
Has gone and who has fulfilled the two requisites[2]
By the power of his spirituality.

From the bottom of my heart, I fold my hands devotedly
To the invincible Lord, Buddha's representative, ⟨2a⟩[3]

---

[1] 'Jam-dbyangs (Mañjughoṣa) is another manifestation of 'Jam-dpal
(Mañjuśri) who has been explained by Mi-pham in his *bShes-sbring gi mchan
'grel padma dkar-po'i phreng-ba* as follows: He is gentle ['jam] because he has
overcome all evil afflictions and he is eternally youthful because his Being
[sku], radiating with the splendor [dpal] of two qualities (of benefitting
oneself and others), never grows old.

[2] The two requisites: the accumulations of profound knowledge and
merits.

[3] Figures in diagonals (eg. ⟨2a⟩) indicate the beginning of each Tibetan
folio.

Known as Maitreyanātha[4] in all the three times
Because he showers his love on all beings.

I bow to the most supreme leaders from among the
Six ornaments of India,[5] renowned as the Great
  Charioteers[6]
Who, having been predicted by the Sugata himself,
Illumined the auspicious Buddha Teachings, profound
  and vast.

I bow to 'Jam-mgon Lama[7] worthy of praise
Like the Buddha-sun to unfold again and let bloom forth
The forest of Sūtras, Tantras, and commentaries,
Like the thousand-petalled lotus, in this country
Surrounded by snow-capped mountains.

May the light of the sun-like reverend Guru
Reside forever in the petal of the lotus-like heart ⟨2a⟩
Brightening the mental eye
That views the auspicious path
By merely seeing a ray of his charismatic activity.

Even if others do not benefit from talk by people like me,
I am dealing here with the mind and mental events
Because I have been urged by others and because
I want to increase the training of my own mind.

---

[4] Maitreyanātha (he whose master is Maitreya): In the Western world, more commonly known as Asaṅga. Asaṅga styled himself Maitreyanātha in order to show his respect to his teacher, Maitreya. Maitreya, who at one time was the human teacher of Asaṅga, became identified with the future Buddha bearing the same name.

[5] The six ornaments of India are Nāgārjuna, Āryadeva, Asaṅga, Vasubandhu, Dignāga, and Dharmakīrti.

[6] The great charioteers are Nāgārjuna, the promoter of the Madhyamika, and Asaṅga, the promoter of the Yogācāra.

[7] 'Jam-mgon Lama refers to Tsong-kha-pa who is considered to be an incarnation of Mañjughoṣa.

Introduction to
Mind and Mental Events

Those intelligent people who are not content with merely acquiring food and clothing as long as they exist in this world, but take into account a future life by thinking what might become of them in the next world, should consider what is the root of their experiencing uninterrupted frustration by being driven around helplessly in *saṃsāra* extending over the three world spheres since beginningless time. Considering the matter in this way, they should realize that the frustration of this world does not come without having a cause or from having a cause that is not appropriate to it, but that it comes from its inherent cause which is man's own actions (*karma*) and the emotions. Nāgārjuna states,

> As long as there is the belief in the *skandhas*,[8]
> There will come from them ⟨3a⟩ a belief in a self.
> When there is a belief in an ego, then there is *karma*.
> From this, there will come (re)birth.

---

[8] *Skandha* is the Indian term for the five psycho-physical constituents: color-form, feeling (judgments), concepts and conceptual process, motivation, and consciousness in the specific sense of perception.

And (MMK. XXV, 10),

> The root of *saṃsāra* is motivation.
> Therefore, the wise do not make plans.
> The unwise, therefore, become agents
> Because they see only unwiseness.

And Āryadeva states (Catuḥśataka, XIV, 25a,b),

> The seeds for the possible world are concepts.
> The objects are their field of activity.

And Candrakīrti states,

> It has been stated that the Mind truly establishes
> In manifold ways the world of sentient beings and
> The world as their container.
> All beings without exception have come from *karma*.

And Vasubandhu states (Abhidharmakoṣa, IV, 1a),

> The various worlds have come from *karma*.

And (Abhidharmakoṣa, V, 1a),

> The basis of existence are the six latent and overt
>   (emotions).

Thus has it been stated many times.
> Moreover, the *spyod-'jug* (Bodhicaryāvatāra, V, 6) states,

> The Buddha himself said, "Thus, all terror
> And also the countless frustrations
> Come from the mind."

And (Bodhicaryāvatāra, V, 17, 18a,b),

> When one does not know the mystery of the mind
> Which is the most important thing regarding the *dharma* ⟨3b⟩,
> But wishes to gain happiness and to relinquish pain,
> He is hopelessly lost; therefore,
> I will properly take hold of and guard my mind.

Again it is said (Bodhicaryāvatāra, VII, 41–45),

> Pain, an unhappy mind, the various terrors,
> And separation from what one cherishes
> Originate from acting in an evil manner.

> Whatever good one does by intending it, turns,
> Wherever one may go, into positive merits and
> Will be respected in virtue of this outcome.

> An evil doer, even if he desires happiness, will,
> By his evil, wherever he goes, be overcome
> By the sword of suffering.

> Dwelling in the heart of a noble, fragrant, beautiful,
>   cool lotus,
> Having splendid health by the food of hearing the
>   Buddha's voice,
> Possessing a glorious body born of the noble lotus by
>   the light of Enlightenment,
> The Sons of the Buddha dwell in the presence of the
>   Victorious One by their own goodness.

> Weakened through flaying by the attendants of
>   the Lord of death,[9]
> And having copper, melted by a scorching fire, poured
>   over one's body, and then
> Having been cut into hundreds of small pieces by a
>   flaming sword moving to and fro,
> The evil doer falls to the ground of blazing iron
>   due to his many evil deeds.

Just as it has been expressed above, it has been said not only once, but over and over again in the Sūtras and Tantras together with their commentaries, ⟨4a⟩ that the whole of *saṃsāra*, the living beings and their world, have come from

---

[9] For the various concepts of hell, see H. V. Guenther, *The Jewel Ornament of Liberation*, pp. 57–62.

their inherent cause which is the power of *karma* and the emotions. So also, it has been said that the infinite qualities of the spiritual levels, the path of the three spiritual pursuits,[10] their result which is Buddhahood, and the Buddha's charismatic activity have come from a positive mind as their inherent cause; and, therefore, the root of the whole of *saṃsāra* and *nirvāṇa* is mind.

Thus, it is essential to know what is meant by mind and mental events. Here in this brief analysis of mind and mental events, there are two parts:

1. Mind and mental events distinguished as to their individual nature and differentiation, and
2. A summary for making a living experience of what is gained by the analysis.

---

[10] The three spiritual pursuits are the Śrāvakayāna, Pratyekayāna, and Bodhisattvayāna. For a detailed explanation, see H. V. Guenther, *Buddhist Philosophy in Theory and Practice.*

Mind and Mental Events Distinguished as to their Individual Nature and Differentiation

Concerning the distinction between mind and mental events, the *dbus-mtha'* (Madhyāntavibhāga, I, 8) states,

> Seeing a thing belongs to mind.
> Seeing its specific characteristic belongs to
> a mental event.

And the *mngon-pa mdzod* (Abhidharmakoṣa, I, 16a) says,

> Consciousness is a selecting awareness.

Accordingly, to be aware of the mere facticity and haecceity of an object is mind, and, on the basis of this objective reference, to become involved with the object by way of other specific functions is said to be the (operation of the) mental events.

The statement of the learned rGyal-tshab[11]—"When sensory perception takes hold of a color patch (complex) as its major concern, there is a singling out process regarding the

---

[11] rGyal-tshab Dharma Rin-chen was a close disciple of Tsong-kha-pa and his immediate successor.

object"—⟨4b⟩ was not made with reference to gaining certainty, but merely with reference to the (apprehension of) color form. In the wake of this operation of mind, mental events have the function of directing the mind towards the object on the basis of the objective reference and the function of other special operations such as not forgetting that which has been understood previously. Therefore, the mind as a primary operation is concerned only with the objective reference but not with what the other specific functions perform; a mental event is an awareness which gets involved with this object by way of other specific functions, such as those following the operation, that deal with the objective reference.

Someone may think, "Are mind and mental events one and the same stuff or are they different?" The *mngon-pa mdzod* (Abhidharmakoṣa, II, 23) has the answer:

The mind and mental events are certainly together.

It has been said that mind as the primary factor and the mental events as its entourage are of one stuff and co-existent by way of the five functional co-relations. Thus, since mind and mental events arise together, as far as time is concerned, and are of one and the same stuff and not of different kinds of stuff, it is inadmissible to claim that mind and mental events are not co-existent in time and are different entities and that they separately deal with their objects. Let me explain this further. When there is memory, or inspection of an object like a colored patch, both mind as the primary factor and its attendant function, memory, correspond to each other in their reference to their object which is this color patch. But their separate functions ⟨5a⟩ consist in the fact that the mind is merely concerned with the facticity and haecceity of the object, while, in view of its function of not forgetting (or losing sight of it), mind is spoken of as memory-inspection [dran-pa]. But these two (mind and mental event) are not separate entities as are a pillar and a jar.

This explanation is based on the *chos mngon rgya mtsho'i snying po* which is an explanation of the *chos mngon-pa kun-las btus-pa* (Abhidharmasamuccaya). According to the *tshad ma rigs rgyan* (Pramāṇavartikālaṃkara),

> The defining characteristic of the mind as the primary factor is to be in union with its attendant mental event by way of the five functional co-relations, and the defining characteristic of mental events is to be in union with the mind as the primary factor by way of the five functional co-relations.

These five functional co-relations are dealt with in the *mngon-pa mdzod* (Abhidharmakośa) and the *mngon-pa kun-btus* (Abhidharmasamuccaya).[12]

The *mngon-pa mdzod* (Abhidharmakośa, II 34d) says that the five functional co-relations are:

1. Alike basis [rten-mtshungs]
2. Alike objective reference [dmigs mtshungs]
3. Alike observable quality [rnam mtshungs]
4. Alike time [dus mtshungs]
5. Alike stuff [rdzas mtshungs]

The meaning of each of them is as follows:

Alike basis means that the sense faculties depend on a mental attitude [sems], so the mental events are alike in this way.

Alike objective reference means that the mental events have the same objective reference as the one taken up by mind.

Alike observable quality means when the mind has a blue content, then the mental events are bluish in content.

Alike time means the mind and mental events arise, stay and fade simultaneously. ⟨5b⟩

---

[12] See the collected works of dPal-sprul O-rgyan 'Jigs-med chos kyi dbang-po in the *Nga Gyur Nyingmay Sungrab*, Vol. 41, pp. 121–22. The *Abhidharmasamuccaya* does not give the list exactly as quoted here. Ye-shes rgyal-mtshan simply summarizes it into the five.

Alike stuff means of whatever stuff a mental attitude may be, the same stuff is the mental event; for example, feeling.

Now the *mngon-pa kun-btus* (Abhidharmasamuccaya, p. 33–34) says that the five functional co-relations are:

1. Alike stuff [rdzas mtshungs-pa]
2. Alike objective reference [dmigs mtshungs]
3. Alike fact [rnam mtshungs]
4. Alike time [dus mtshungs]
5. Alike spheres and levels [khams dang sa mtshungs-pa]

Alike stuff means that in the entourage of one attitude as the primary factor, there is only one corresponding mental event such as feeling because two different corresponding events cannot take place.

Alike objective reference and *alike fact* means that as the observable quality and its presence can have only one objective reference, and as according to this objective reference and observable quality there is either an emotional coloring or not, when mind as the primary factor becomes emotionally tainted, so do the mental events as its entourage. But when the mind becomes such that it is not affected by what otherwise is bound to break [zag-med],[13] the mental events as its entourage become such that they are not affected by what otherwise is bound to break.

Alike time means the mind as a primary factor and mental events as its attendants arise, stay, and fade simultaneously.

Alike spheres and levels means when the mind as primary factor is on the level of *kāmadhātu* (world of desire), the mental events belonging to the sphere of the *rūpadhātu* (world of form)

---

[13] The Tibetan term *zag-med* (what otherwise is bound to break) is a difficult term and refers to anything that breaks down the moment we try to build on it. For example, only too often we assume that something could not happen to us, but it does and takes us unaware; then our whole world collapses.

or the *arūpyadhātu* (world of no form) cannot arise as its entourage; and for a mind on the level of *rūpadhātu*, mental events belonging to the *kāmadhātu* cannot arise as its entourage. To whichever sphere a mind belongs, it is on this sphere also ⟨6a⟩ that the mental events as its entourage must arise.

MIND [SEMS]

As to the mind, the *phung-po lnga'i rab-byed* (Pañca-skandhaprakaraṇa, P. ed. 113, p. 238, 5.6) states,

> What is perception? It is a distinct awareness of what is before the mind.

The *mngon-pa mdzod* (Abhidharmakoṣa, I, 16) states,

> Perception is a process of singling out.

The learned rGyal-tshab declares,

> The individualizing perception by means of being aware of the mere factual presence of an object is the defining characteristic of the mind.

When one analyses perception, one finds that there are six patterns.[14] The *mngon-pa kun-las-btus* (Abhidharmasamuccaya, p. 12) states,

> What is perception? There are six patterns: visual perception, auditory perception, olfactory perception, taste perception, tactile perception, and categorical perception.
>
> What is *visual perception*? It is a function of selecting color-form as its objective reference. This takes place in the eye.
>
> What is *auditory perception*? It is a function of selecting sound as its objective reference. It takes place in the ear.

---

[14] See also *mkhas-'jug*, fol. 10b–11a.

What is *olfactory perception*? It is a function of selecting smell as its objective reference. It takes place in the nose.

What is *taste perception*? It is a function of selecting taste as its objective reference. It takes place in the tongue.

What is *tactile perception*? It is a function of selecting touch as its objective reference. It takes place in the skin.

What is *categorical perception*? It is a function of selecting out conceptualized contents [chos dmigs]. It takes place in the mind ⟨6b⟩.

Although there seem to be many specific distinctions in the earlier and later philosophical systems concerning the three conditions of these six perceptual functions, they are not dealt with here.

It is true that Asaṅga and his brother (Vasubandhu) speak in their works about the *ālayavijñāna* and *kliṣṭamanovijñāna*.[15] But I will write in a general way about mind and mental events in so far as they are absolutely necessary for our knowledge of how one's actions (*karma*) and emotions tie one to *saṃsāra* when, in view of the states on the path to Enlightenment, a person who is on an intermediary level thinks about the evils of *saṃsāra* and how they come about. The question whether there is an *ālayavijñāna* or not poses a very great and specific problem in the later and earlier philosophical systems. Asaṅga and his brother who follow the *dgongs-pa rjes 'grel* (Sandhinirmocanasūtra) divide the Buddha Word into implicit and explicit

---

[15] *Ālayavijñāna* [kun-gzhi rnam-par shes-pa] is a pervasive medium capable of retaining traces of experiences and their structures which may become actual experiences under suitable conditions. It is certainly not a mind. To associate it with perceptual processes collectively called 'consciousness' or 'mind' (*vijñāna*), as is done in the Indian Yogācāra system, is a continuation of concretistic thinking. In rNying-ma-pa thought, the *ālayavijñāna* is clearly distinct from the *ālaya* and the former is seen as a move towards a subject's mind. *Kliṣṭamanovijñāna* indicates the emotionally toned reaction that goes with our categorical or conceptual perceptions. For example, we perceive visually a green patch and conceptually a tree to which we react positively, negatively, or indifferently.

statements and posit an *ālayavijñāna*. They declare the whole of reality to be of the nature of mere mentation [sems tsam gyi bdag-nyid].

Nāgārjuna and Āryadeva, who follow the *ting nge 'dzin rgyal pa'i mdo* (Samādhirājasūtra) and the *blo-gros mi-zad-pa'i mdo* (Akṣayamatiparipṛcchasūtra), also divide the Buddha Word into the explicit and implicit statements but do not accept an *ālayavijñāna*. They explain the Sūtras that deal with an *ālayavijñāna* as having an implicit meaning and state that the whole of reality is a set of logical fictions [drang don dgongs pa can].

Therefore, in the holy land of India, ⟨7a⟩ there are two great trends in the Mahāyāna. These do not differ in their intention insofar as it concerns the development of the Enlightenment attitude and the practice of the six *pāramitās* (perfections).[16] There is only a difference in philosophical thinking. In spite of this difference, neither of these two great leaders, Nāgārjuna or Asaṅga, is superior or inferior as far as his philosophical thinking goes. As has been made clear by the Buddha himself in many Sūtras, these two ways of elucidation correspond to the individual understanding of those who have to be guided.

Therefore, if you want to know more deeply the specific points in the teaching of Asaṅga and his brother positing an *ālayavijñāna* and by implication establishing the whole of reality as being of mentation only, you should look up the works of Asaṅga and his brother as well as Tsong-kha-pa's *legs-bshad*. If you want to know the specific points of Nāgārjuna's thought, you should look up those works which are so valuable in the three worlds, the *lhag mthong* and the *rtsa 'jug gi rnam* of Tsong-kha-pa.

---

[16] The six *pāramitās* are liberality, ethics, patience, strenuousness, meditative concentration, and appreciative discrimination. See H. V. Guenther, *The Jewel Ornament of Liberation*, p. 148 ff.

MENTAL EVENTS [SEMS-BYUNG]

In the discussion of the mental events, the *phung-po lnga'i rab byed* (Pañcaskandhaprakaraṇa, P. ed. 113, p. 237, 4.4) states the nature of mental events as follows ⟨7b⟩:

> What are mental events? They are whatever correspond to the mind.

When these mental events are classified, there are fifty-one:

1. Five ever present ones beginning with feeling-tone
2. Five object-determining ones beginning with interest
3. Eleven positive ones beginning with confidence-trust
4. Six basic emotions beginning with cupidity-attachment
5. Twenty proximate emotions beginning with indignation
6. Four variables beginning with drowsiness

The *phung-po lnga'i rab-byed* (Pañcaskandhaprakaraṇa, P. ed. 113, p. 237, 5.1–5.2) states:

1. Five are omnipresent.
2. Five are always certain about any object which becomes their domain.
3. Eleven are positive (ie. only operate in positive attitudes).
4. Six are the (basic) emotions (ie. they are upsetting and, by coloring one's view, make clarity of mind turbulent).
5. The remaining are proximate.
6. Four are variable.

The Five Omnipresent Mental Events [kun 'gro lnga][17]

The five omnipresent mental events (that operate in the wake of every mind situation) are:

1. Feeling-tone [tshor-ba]
2. Conceptualization ['du-shes]
3. Directionality of mind [sems-pa][18]
4. Rapport [reg-pa][19]
5. Egocentric demanding [yid la byed-pa][20]

Feeling-tone [tshor-ba]

In the *mngon-pa kun-las-btus* (Abhidharmasamuccaya, p. 2), the nature of feeling is explained as follows:

> What is the absolutely specific characteristic of feeling? It is to experience. That is to say, in any experience, what we experience is the individual maturation of any positive or negative action as its final result.

Here, the experience of feeling is called maturation. This is said for the purpose of becoming aware of the fact that pleasant or unpleasant feelings arising in us are nothing more than the result of the maturation of our action. The *lam-rim chen-mo* explains this as follows:

> The infallibility of our actions means that, whether we be ordinary persons ⟨8a⟩ or exalted beings, any pleasure with its

---

[17] *mkhas-'jug*, fol 5b–6a.

[18] *sems-pa*, directionality of mind, agitates the mind and lets it get involved with the object. Dealing with it from the basis from which it operates, it is the whole complex. When we see something, as in visual perception, our mind goes in the direction of the object.

[19] Sensory activity cannot change, thus, it is the basis from which we have feeling-tones.

[20] Holding the mind on what it has so selected, ie. its objective reference. It is fixation, ideation, and mental adhesion. See *mkhas-'jug*, fol. 61a,b.

pleasant feeling tone which occurs in us or any feeling of relief as is felt in a cool breeze by those born in hell, starts from previously accumulated positive actions, for it is impossible for pleasure to come from negative actions. So also, every painful feeling, even if it may occur in a saintly person, comes from previously accumulated negative actions, for it is impossible for pain to come from positive actions. The *rin chen 'phreng-ba* (Ratnamala) states,

> From negative actions come all frustrations
> And also, all evil forms of life.
> From positive actions come all happy forms of life,
> And also, all happiness in every walk of life.

Therefore, pleasure and frustration do not originate without a cause nor do they originate from inappropriate causes such as the gods Viṣṇu, Śiva, or anyone else. From generally positive or negative actions come generally positive or negative feelings. The various shades of these feelings come from the intensity of positive or negative actions. In each case, the certainty that the relationship between one's action and its result is certain and infallible, with no irregularity whatsoever, is the right view held by all Buddhists and praised as the foundation of all that is bright.

Feeling is classified as pleasant, unpleasant, and indifferent. The *phung-po lnga'i rab-byed* (Pañcaskandhaprakaraṇa, P. ed. 113, p. 237, 3.6–4.2) ⟨8b⟩ states,

> What is feeling? It is three ways of experiencing—pleasantly, unpleasantly, and indifferently. 'Pleasant' is that which one would like to feel again (when the original feeling is over). 'Unpleasant' is what one would like to get rid of when it is present. 'Indifferent' is where neither of these two desires occur.

These three feelings become six according to their division whether they occur physically or mentally so that one has three physical feelings and three mental feelings.

The three physical feelings are: physically pleasant, physically unpleasant, and physically indifferent.

The three mental feelings are: mentally pleasant, mentally unpleasant, and mentally indifferent.

The difference between physical and mental feelings is that physical feelings occur within the realm of the five sense perceptions while mental feelings are those which occur in the realm of thought.

Why do we talk about physical feeling as that which occurs within the realm of sense perception? The *bzhi brgya pa* (Catuḥśataka) says,

> Darkness is everywhere just as the skin covers the whole body.

Since the skin covers the whole body from head to toe, feelings which originate in the realm of the other four sensory perceptions are also called ⟨9a⟩ physical feelings.

If we further distinguish those six feelings as subjectivistic feelings and transpersonal feelings, we have an additional twelve which make up a total of eighteen. Subjectivistic feelings are those that are always on the level of thinking that they are *my* feelings, while the transpersonal feelings are those which are felt on the level of primal awareness which immediately understands that there is no abiding principle to which the self may be reduced.

You might ask how it is that those who have this primal awareness by which they immediately understand that the self is not an eternal entity, have painful feelings, since the transpersonal feeling just explained would be in the realm of frustration. Oh, there are many reasons for this. For example, the *'dul-ba lung* (Vinayaśāstra) states,

> Even those Arhats who have rejected the belief that self is an eternal entity still suffer such unpleasant feelings as headaches as a result of their former actions.

There are six feelings according to their location:

1. Feelings which occur in the rapport established by the eye

  2. Feelings which occur in the rapport established by the ear
  3. Feelings which occur in the rapport established by the nose
  4. Feelings which occur in the rapport established by the tongue
  5. Feelings which occur from the rapport established by the body
  6. Feelings which occur from the rapport established by the mind

Since each ⟨9b⟩ one of these six can be pleasant, unpleasant, or indifferent, one can speak of eighteen feelings. If I were to deal with these in detail, it would be too lengthy, so I shall stop here.

Feeling classified according to the function of rejection and aiding is twofold:

  1. A sustaining feeling of addiction
  2. A sustaining feeling of realization

The sustaining feeling of addiction occurs on the level of desiring sensuous things of this world. The sustaining feeling of realization is to turn away from being addicted to these things and occurs on the level of those thought processes which are summarized by the subject matter of the first meditative stage.[21]

This division into two kinds of feelings is made here for the purpose of knowing how the strength of feeling itself may, on the one hand, bring to light an existing desire or bring about detachment from this addiction through the subject matter of meditative concentration. But if one wants to know this more deeply, one should look up the *Abhidharmakoṣa*, the *Abhidharmasamuccaya*, and also the *byang-chub lam-rim* in order to prevent the three feelings of pleasure, pain, and indifference from becoming the cause of the three poisons.[22]

---

[21] See H. V. Guenther, *The Jewel Ornament of Liberation*, p. 80.

[22] The three poisons are cupidity-attachment (*rāga*), aversion-hatred (*dveṣa*), and bewilderment-erring (*moha*).

Conceptualization [*'du-shes*][23]

In the *mngon-pa kun-las-btus* (Abhidharmasamuccaya, p. 2), the nature of conceptualization is stated as follows:

> What is the absolutely specific characteristic of conceptualization? It is to know by association. ⟨10a⟩ It is to see, hear, specify, and to know by way of taking up the defining characteristics and distinguishing them.

It is an awareness that deals with the specific characteristic of an object when the object, sensory capacity, and cognitive act have joined.

And in the *phung-po lnga rab-byed* (Pañcaskandha-prakaraṇa, P. ed. 113, p. 237, 4.2) it is explained as follows:

> What is conceptualization? It is taking hold of the defining characteristic of an object.

Conceptualization is twofold:

1. Dealing with the defining characteristic
2. Dealing with the specific characteristic

The former deals with the specific characteristic of an apparent object in a conceptless perception and the latter deals with the specific characteristic of an apparent object in a judgmental perception.

The bases for the operation of these two forms of conceptualization are seeing, hearing, specification (differentiation), and full cognition. Their meanings are:

To see is to make a proposition about what has been seen in immediate perception.

To hear is to make a proposition on the basis of trustworthy information.

Differentiation means to make a proposition about an object which is ascertained as this or that object in view of its characteristics.

---

[23] See *mkhas-'jug*, fol. 5a.

Full cognition is to make a proposition by way of concept about this object as it is, in the certainty of immediate perception.

The *mngon-pa mdzod* (Abhidharmakoṣa, I, 14c,d) explains the two aspects of conceptualization as the defining characteristic and as propositions. That is to say, the former is to distinguish the individual color design such as blue, yellow etc., and the other is to distinguish the individual propositional form in making such statements as, "This is a man" and "This is a woman."[24] ⟨10b⟩

Conceptualization is sixfold[25] according to the basis from which it operates. That is,

1. Those that start from the rapport that exists in visual perception
2. Those that start from the rapport that exists in auditory perception
3. Those that start from the rapport that exists in olfactory perception
4. Those that start from the rapport that exists in gustatory perception
5. Those that start from the rapport that exists in tactile perception
6. Those that start from the rapport that exists in ideational (thought) perception

It is again sixfold in view of its reference.

1. Conceptualization which has defining characteristics
2. Conceptualization which does not have defining characteristics

---

[24] The author obviously tries to give an analysis of a perceptual situation indicated by the phrase "I see a woman." This is to say that there is an objective constituent which displays certain qualities that there is in a perceptual situation an objective constituent which we believe of the proposition "This is a woman." This belief of course does not guarantee that there is an ontological object of the physical object corresponding to the epistemological object of the perceptual situation.

[25] See *mkhas-'jug*, fol. 5a.

3. Conceptualization which is limited
4. Conceptualization which is broader
5. Conceptualization which is infinite
6. Conceptualization which is nothing whatsoever

The first ('conceptualization which has defining characteristics') is threefold:

1. One in which one knows the coherence between names and things
2. One which refers to the fact that everything composite is transitory
3. One which clarifies this reference

The second is also threefold in view of the fact that it is opposite to the previous ones.

'Limited conceptualization' refers to the ideas of those who are concerned only with the pleasures of this world and to all those ideas of the ordinary people who are in the world of desire and who have not reached the subject matter of meditation.

The 'broader viewpoint' refers to those ideas found in those who are on the level of aesthetic perception and to the concepts referring to the aesthetic world perception.

The 'infinite viewpoint' ⟨11a⟩ refers to those ideas that deal with an experience that is wide and open like the infinite sky and the experience of the unlimitedness of the cognitive capacity.

The sixth is the idea of an experience which one would objectify as nothing.[26]

Directionality of mind [*sems-pa*][27]

In the *mngon-pa kun-las-btus* (Abhidharmasamuccaya, p. 2), the nature of directionality of mind is described as follows:

---

[26] See *mkhas-'jug*, fol. 5a and 28a,b.

[27] See *mkhas-'jug*, fol. 5b. *sems-pa* refers to the total psychic energy. It is motivating force.

What is directionality? It is a mental activity that propels the mind forward. It has the function of making the mind settle on what is positive, negative, or indeterminate.

It is a mental event that arouses and urges the mind with its corresponding events on towards an object.

From among all mental events, it is said to be the most important because the force of this mental event sets the mind and any mental event on to the object. Just as iron cannot but be attracted by a magnet, so also the mind cannot be but set on an object by this mental event.

It is sixfold in view of the basis from which it operates:

1. Directionality occurring in visual situations
2. Directionality occurring in auditory situations
3. Directionality occurring in olfactory situations
4. Directionality occurring in gustatory situations
5. Directionality occurring in tactile situations
6. Directionality occurring in thought situations

While this directionality is a mental operation, action ⟨11b⟩ is twofold insofar as it is directionality and intentionality.

The *mngon-pa mdzod* (Abhidharmakoṣa, IV, 1c,d) states,

> Action is directionality and what has been set up by it.
> That which has been set up are bodily and verbal acts.

Intentional activity takes place in bodily and verbal actions. Although they are unlimited, in summarizing their most important features, there are seven in reference to actions by body and speech and ten in reference to actions in a social context. Therefore, the *mdzod* (Abhidharmakoṣa, IV, 66) states,

> From a broad viewpoint,
> The paths of action are said to be ten
> According to their being wholesome and unwholesome.

The classification of actions is threefold: positive, negative, and indeterminate; or, meritorious, non-meritorious, and neutral.

It is very important to know well the differentiation of how to recognize these actions and how their effects come about, how they project (a life style) and bring about its fulfillment, how they are to be experienced with certainty and without certainty, how in the way of being experienced with certainty they are experienced immediately, indirectly, or in the future; but it would be too much to go into these details. Those who are eager and intelligent will know them when they study the *Abhidharmakoṣa* and its commentary by the great scholar Vasubandhu and ⟨12a⟩ the *legs bshad dri ma med pa* by Tsong-kha-pa.

Rapport [*reg-pa*][28]

The *mngon-pa kun-las-btus* (Abhidharmasamuccaya, p. 6) explains rapport as follows:

> What is rapport? It is a determination, a transformation in the controlling power, which is in accordance with the three factors coming together. Its function is to provide a basis for feeling.

It is an awareness in which a pleasant feeling is felt when the object, sensory capacity, and cognitive process have come together and which is restricted to the appropriate object. Transformation in the controlling power means that when the visual sense meets a pleasant object and the feeling becomes the cause of adhering to this pleasure, rapport restricts the pleasant color-form and the feeling becomes the cause of pleasure.

According to its operation, rapport is sixfold:

1. Rapport with visual situations
2. Rapport with auditory situations

---

[28] *mkhas-'jug*, fol. 6a.

3. Rapport with olfactory situations
4. Rapport with gustatory situations
5. Rapport with tactile situations
6. Rapport with thought situations

Egocentric demanding [*yid la byed-pa*][29]

The *mgnon-pa kun-las-btus* (Abhidharmasamuccaya, p. 6) explains egocentric demanding as follows:

> What is egocentric demanding? It is a continuity having the function of holding the mind to what has become its reference.

It is a cognition that keeps the complex of mind in its specific objective reference.

The difference between directionality and egocentric demanding is that directionality brings the mind towards the object in a general move ⟨12b⟩, while egocentric demanding makes the mind jump on this particular objective reference.

The reason for speaking of these five mental events, beginning with feeling-tone as omnipresent, is that they are lumped together because they are events that operate in the wake of every mind situation.

Moreover, if any one of the five omnipresent mental events is missing, the experience of the object is incomplete. If there is no feeling-tone, there is no relishing of it. If there is no conceptualization, one does not get the specific characteristic of the object. If there is no directionality of mind, there is no getting on to the object. If there is no rapport, there would be no basis for perception. If there is no egocentric demanding, then the various objects would not be confronted. Hence, in order to have a complete appreciation and enjoyment of an object, these five omnipresent mental events must be there altogether, completely and fully.

---

[29] *mkhas-'jug*, fol. 6a.

The Five Object-determining Mental Events [yul nges lnga]³⁰

The five object-determining mental events are:

1. Interest ['dun-pa]
2. Intensified interest which stays with its object [mos-pa]
3. Inspection (to learn more) [dran-pa]
4. Intense concentration [ting-nge-'dzin]³¹
5. Appreciative discrimination [shes-rab]

Interest ['dun-pa]

The *mngon-pa kun-las-btus* (Abhidharmasamuccaya, p. 6) explains the nature of interest as follows:

> What is interest? It is the desire to endow a desired thing with this or that particular attribute, and has the function of laying the foundation for making a start on assiduous striving.

It is an awareness which gets involved with the intended object.

The way of laying the foundation for making a start on assiduous striving is explained in the *dbus mtha'* (Madhyānta-vibhāga, IV, 5a,b) as follows:

> The occasion, that which depends on it, and their cause and effect relationship.³²

The *lam-rim chen-mo* states,

> If one is unable to suppress laziness which delights in the non-inclination towards the practice of meditation and which delights in the factors not conducive to the practice, then one quickly loses all interest because first of all ⟨13a⟩ one does not allow the mind to go into concentration and, even if one

---

³⁰ See *mkhas-'jug*, fol. 6a.
³¹ See *mkhas-'jug*, fol. 71b, 79a.
³² See Mi-pham's *dbus dang mtha' rnam par 'byed pa'i bstan bcos kyi 'grel pa 'od zer phreng ba*, fol. 30a.

should attain concentration, one cannot maintain its continuity. Therefore, at the very beginning it is most important to overcome laziness. When one has attained a state of alertness which is satiated happiness and pleasure both on the physical and mental level, and when one is not weary to apply himself day or night to what is positive, then laziness is overcome. In order to generate this alertness, it is important that one has the concentration which is the sustaining cause of the aforesaid state of alertness and that one makes this a continuous process. In order to have the power of concentration, one must have a strong and continuous involvement in concentration. In order that concentration be a sustaining cause factor, one must repeatedly invoke a firm conviction which enraptures one's whole mind because one has seen the virtues and value of concentration. To understand these qualities and processes in this order must be taken as the most essential point because they become clear and certain in seeing them in one's own experience.

The meaning of the passage, 'the occasion' in the work cited above (Madhyāntavibhāga), is as follows: *occasion* means interest, the starting point of endeavor. *That which depends on it* means endeavor or effort; the *cause*, the sustaining force of interest, means a firm conviction regarding the quality and value of the thing. The *effect* or outcome is alertness.

If one thinks deeply about this in the manner that Tsong-kha-pa has explained, one may discover a special importance attached to his words; however, if one has put into one's mind merely the words of the great charioteers, who state that the progress of the path follows a distinct pattern, one will gain certainty regarding practice; but because one ⟨13b⟩ believes merely the words and thinks only of the arguments and supporting teachings of those great charioteers, he not only rejects the opportunity of practice, and thus loses the opportunity of obtaining certainty about it, but he even loses the opportunity of understanding anything. Just look at how the path in which the Buddhas delight comes to life in oneself!

Interest is threefold:

1. That with which you want to meet
2. That with which you do not want to part
3. That in which you really want to get involved

There are many other involvements of interest such as the involvement with desired things and involvement with what one sees.

Intensified interest which stays with its object [*mos-pa*]

The *mngon-pa kun-btus* (Abhidharmasamuccaya, p. 6) explains the nature of intensified interest which stays with its object as follows:

> What is intensified interest? It is to stick to the determined thing just as it has been determined, and the function of intensified interest is that it cannot be taken away.

It is an awareness by which one stays with what the mind [yul-can] has logically established as this is so and not otherwise.

Here, its specific function has been described in the words, 'it cannot be taken away', because when one has a firm conviction about the object, one is certain and cannot be swayed by anyone. For example, if one thinks about who is the infallible refuge, the Buddha or another, then one will find out that only the Buddha ⟨14a⟩ is the infallible refuge. Then one becomes certain, through valid means of cognition, that the teachings of the Buddha and the community which has realized the teaching are the infallible refuges. Anyone who has this firm conviction cannot be swayed by any other opinion and is counted as a Buddhist. On this basis the bright qualities (of spiritual progress) increase. Therefore, the *spyod-'jug* (Bodhicaryāvatāra, VII, 40) states:

The Buddha has said that
The root of everything positive
Is the intensification of interest.
That root always matures
By producing an effect.

Inspection [dran-pa]

The *mngon-pa kun-las-btus* (Abhidharmasamuccaya, p. 6)
explains the nature of inspection as follows:

> What is inspection? It is not to let what one knows slip away
> from one's mind. Its function is not to be distracted.

It is an awareness which has three specific features:

1. Specific feature of the object—it is a thing you know
2. Specific feature of the observable quality—this object is
   not forgotten
3. Specific feature of the function—it remains steady

Since inspection does not arise concerning a thing which has
not been well known previously, the specific feature of its
function is said to deal with something familiar. Since inspection does not operate on an object which does not come to mind
at present even though it may have been familiar before, it
implies the feature of not letting the object slip out of the mind.
On the basis of this special function, the levels of the mind can
grow in intensity and this means that mind does not swerve
⟨14b⟩.

The fact that inspection must possess the three specific
functions is very important whether one deals with the Sūtras
or Tantras. Therefore, Nāgārjuna (Suhṛllekha, 54) has said,

> The Tathāgata has taught that
> Inspection belonging to the great beings
> Is the only path to walk.
> To this hold tight and preserve it.
> If inspection slips, everything is lost.

The *spyod-'jug* (Bodhicaryāvatāra, V, 26–30) states,

> Those who have listened and have confidence
> But do not apply assiduous striving,
> By being attached to the defect of not knowing properly,
> Will become soiled by falling away from their status.
>
> Those thieves, the lack of awareness and
> The pursuit of that from which inspection slips,
> Not only rob one's wealth and a happy state of existence,
> But they also cause one to wander about
>   in evil existences.
>
> These robbers, which are the emotions,
> Go about seeking an opportunity.
> When they get it, they steal the wholesome
> And even destroy life in a good existence.
>
> Therefore, never, never allow inspection
> To wander out of the mind's door.
> But if by chance it should, then by recalling
> Those pains of evil existence, bring it back close to you.
>
> By keeping company with a guru and
> By the instructions of the learned,
> Those who are pious and pay respect because they
>   are afraid something may go wrong
> Will gain inspection which develops the positive.

All values (qualities) inherent in the various levels and paths depend on inspection and awareness. Since any attainment of concentration, be it on the basis of the Sūtras or Tantras, must be attained by virtue of this specific function, ⟨15a⟩ the application of inspection is very important for those who want to have this experience coming from the bottom of their hearts.

Thus, the *spyod-'jug* (Bodhicaryāvatāra, V, 22–23) states,

> May my possessions, my status,
> My body and my life be for nothing!
> May even all other wholesome things come to nought!
> But, may the mind never be lessened.

To those who desire to guard the mind,
I pray, saying,
"Preserve your inspection and awareness
Even if it costs you your life."

Intense concentration [*ting nge 'dzin*]

The *mngon-pa kun-las-btus* (Abhidharmasamuccaya, p. 6)
explains intense concentration as follows:

> What is intense concentration? It is one-pointedness of mind
> which continues with an idea, and its function is to become the
> basis for awareness [shes-pa].

It is to let the mind continue with its objective reference. The
reason for calling the particular content of intense concentration an idea is that in practicing concentration, one holds the
mind to what is postulated by intellect, and this is an idea.

Moreover, although there are countless things which may
appear as that on which one can concentrate, in brief, there are
four:

1. The objective reference which purifies the conduct of
   life
2. The objective reference which purifies emotions
3. The objective reference which are the (four) encom-
   passing activities (of loving kindness, compassion, joy
   and equanimity)
4. The objective reference with which the wise deal

The objective reference with which the wise deal is said to
be limitless and refers to (such topics as the five) constitutive
elements, the (three) levels of existence, the (six) perceptual
spheres, dependent origination and so on ⟨15b⟩.

Nowadays, some people who take the Buddha's words out
of context and make a display of meditation, meditate by
concentrating on what appears before their visual perception,
but Asaṅga has stated very clearly that concentration does not

take place in sensory perception but in categorical perception, and the objective reference is not the visible object that is present in sensory perception, but its precept.

Now if you think that the object of intense concentration must necessarily be a real object, this is not the case. You can concentrate on anything—be it a real or fictitious object. If you work on it intuitively, you get from it a pure and non-conceptualized vision. The *rnam 'brel* (Pramāṇavārttika) states,

> Whether it is real or not,
> Whatever becomes truly familiar
> When you have become fully conversant with it
> Results in a clear feeling of presence without
>   subject-object dichotomy.

The specific function of intense concentration is said to provide a basis for an awareness in which one has a state of mind settled in itself, (a mind) taking every individual aspect of the perceptual situation as it is and never occurring in a vacuum, even though attention may shift within this perception (from one aspect to another).[33]

The *spyod-'jug* (Bodhicaryāvatāra, VIII, 4) states,

> From having known that the charges of emotions
>   are overcome
> Through a widened perspective which is together
>   with calm ⟨16a⟩,
> One must first become calm, and this comes
> When one is not attached to the world.

The *'dul ba lung* (Vinayaśāstra) states,

> Depending on conduct there is intense concentration,
> And depending on intense concentration, there is
>   appreciative discrimination.

---

[33] H. V. Guenther, "On Spiritual Discipline", *Maitreya*, no. 3, p. 30. "Attention is always a fluctuating process, but its fluctuations can remain strictly within the perception. That is, we may concentrate on one aspect of it and then on another; in each case we will not use attention for meta-perceptual ends, but will find ever new potentialities."

Such statements are made over and over again. Therefore, those who want to have liberation must take these works as the Sublime Instruction.

Appreciative discrimination [*shes-rab*]

The *mngon-pa kun-las-btus* (Abhidharmasamuccaya, p. 6) explains the nature of appreciative discrimination as follows:

> What is appreciative discrimination? It is the distinction of all that which is firmly established. Its function is to avoid any confusion or doubt.

It is an awareness which discriminates between the individual observable qualities and defects as well as between the qualities of what is under consideration. The object which has been singled out by appreciative discrimination is threefold:

1. Positive
2. Negative
3. Indeterminate

and the individual defects and qualities of these are distinguished.

There are four logical procedures by which the individual defects and qualities are distinguished:

1. Awareness of what must be done
2. Awareness of relationship
3. Awareness of attaining proper validity
4. Awareness of the absolute real

Since doubt is dispelled when certainty is attained through an investigation which derives from these four operations, the specific function of discriminative awareness is said to abolish doubt.

In cogitating their respective significance, Tsong-kha-pa states (in the *lam-rim chen-mo*),

> May the investigating mind which ⟨16b⟩
> Arises from thinking, day and night, about

What is before the mind, dispel doubt after
Singling out the significance of what has been heard
By means of the four operations.

The reason that the five mental events beginning with intention are here called 'object-determining' is that these mental events have each grasped the specification of the object. When they are steady, there is certainty concerning each object.

The Eleven Positive Mental Events [dge-ba bcu-gcig][34]

The third, the eleven positive mental events are:
1. Confidence-trust [dad-pa]
2. Self-respect [ngo-tsha]
3. Decorum [khrel-yod-pa]
4. Non-attachment [ma chags-pa]
5. Non-hatred [zhe-sdang med-pa]
6. Non-deludedness [gti-mug med-pa]
7. Diligence [brtson-'grus]
8. Alertness [shin-tu sbyangs-pa]
9. Concern [bag yod]
10. Equanimity [btang-snyoms]
11. Non-violence [rnam-par-mi-'tshe-ba]

Confidence-trust [dad-pa]

The *mngon-pa kun-btus* (Abhidharmasamuccaya, p. 6) explains the nature of confidence-trust as follows:

> What is confidence-trust? It is a deep conviction, lucidity, and longing for those things which are real, have value, and are possible. It functions as the basis of sustained interest.

---

[34] See *mkhas-'jug*, fol. 6a.

It is an awareness that counteracts lack of trust through three aspects of trust, namely, deep conviction, lucidity, and longing trust.

Confidence-trust is of three kinds:

1. Lucid confidence [dang-ba'i dad-pa]
2. Trusting confidence [yid ches gyi dad-pa]
3. Longing confidence [mngon 'dod gyi dad-pa]

Lucid confidence is a lucid mind. It is an attitude that comes when one has seen the worth of such valuables as the Three Jewels (Buddha, Dharma and Saṇgha). ⟨17a⟩ When one puts a water-purifying gem into murky water, it becomes limpid immediately. So when this confidence is born, the turbidities of the mind become limpid and all the values of real understanding can grow in one.

Trusting confidence is trust which arises from thinking about the connection that exists between one's action and its result as taught by the Buddha.

Longing confidence is the thought that, having pondered over the four truths, those of frustration and of its origin have to be given up, and those of the cessation and of the way to it have certainly to be realized. When we know that through our efforts these truths can be realized, we certainly will do so.

Here we have only touched upon the nature of the three kinds of confidence-trust, but they are not exhausted thereby.

At present, people lump pleasure and confidence-trust together. We may say that the pleasure in drinking wine is a trust in the wine, but the pleasure and trust certainly are not one and the same. Trust is a mental event which is essentially positive, but pleasure shares in what is positive and negative.

Moreover, in explaining these two in greater detail, we have four alternatives:

1. Liking something but not trusting
2. Trusting but not liking
3. Both
4. Neither

The first, 'liking something but not trusting': you may like your son and wife (but not trust them), and you may like such activities as drinking wine and eating food at inappropriate times ⟨17b⟩.

The second, 'trusting but not liking': you may have a strong conviction from a deep fear of the evils of *saṃsāra* (and hence not like it).

Both liking and trusting is joyful trust that comes from a deep conviction after having pondered over the positive results deriving from positive actions and (from having pondered) on the value of spiritual friends.

Neither liking nor trusting is like anger and frustration.

Now then, are pleasures and personal feelings the same or different? We can say in some sense they are one and the same but actually they are not. To like a spiritual friend is a trust, but the personal feeling of respect regarding that spiritual friend is a distinct mental event which is produced in one's being. It is to feel humble and to cherish this feeling by thinking of what he has done for you. And these are two different mental events.

When someone in his individual awareness deeply questions this according to the great treatise [*lam-rim*], and when he analyzes how it grows in him when he turns the mind inward, then he can know what is meant. Mere words cannot explain this.

In view of this topic, the all-knowing (Tsong-kha-pa) has repeatedly stated that in order to experience this from the bottom of one's being, one has to associate with wise spiritual friends and become very familiar with what the teachings have to say. But, when these great treatises are explained, today's fools, poor in intelligence and low in their stock of merits, become frightened ⟨18a⟩ and turn away from them like a poisonous snake catching the smell of musk or like a small child running away upon seeing the surging ocean. Those who realize the works of the Sages and sublime persons of India as the very foundation of instructions are like stars in daytime.

The statement that the function of trust is to provide a basis for (sustained) interest means that the basis of all (positive) qualities is endeavor, and that for the birth of endeavor an interest which is involved with the problem is necessary. For the birth of such interest, there must be the vision of its qualities and a trusting confidence in all teachings and their commentaries; thus, confidence-trust has been said to be the foundation of all qualities.

So also, the *dkon mchog ta la'i gzungs* (Ratnōlkānāmadhāraṇi) states,

> Confidence must precede all things like a mother (her child).
> It guards and increases all positive things.
> It removes fears and rescues from the (four) rivers.[35]
> Confidence is the road sign to the citadel of happiness.
>
> Confidence is not murky and makes the mind translucent.
> It removes arrogance and becomes the root of devotion.
> Confidence is wealth, treasure, and the best foundation.
> Like the hand, it is the means for gathering what is wholesome.

And the *chos bcu pa* says,

> Wherever one may arrive at by being led,
> Confidence is the best vehicle.
> Therefore, the intelligent person
> Sticks close to confidence.
>
> In people without confidence,
> Positive qualities are not produced, ⟨18b⟩
> Just as a seed consumed by fire
> Cannot become a green sprout.

Thus, it has been stated that all bright qualities come in the wake of confidence-trust, and so the statement, 'where the root of confidence is made firm', in the *bslab btus* (Śikṣasamuccaya)

---

[35] The four rivers or four floods are: flood of sensuality, flood of existence, flood of opinion, and flood of unknowing. See *Abhidharmakoṣa*, V, 37.

explains that confidence-trust is the foundation of all the paths. The great personality and teacher Nāgārjuna also states in the *byang chub lam gyi rim pa*'s table of content,

> The root is the development of confidence.
> The root of everything happy is this trusting confidence.

Self-respect [ngo-tsha shes-pa]

The *mngon-pa kun-btus* (Abhidharmasamuccaya, p. 6) explains self-respect as follows:

> What is self-respect? It is to avoid what is objectionable as far as I see it and its function is to provide a basis for refraining from evil behavior.

It is to refrain from what is objectionable by having made oneself the norm.

Decorum [khrel yod-pa]

The *mngon-pa kun-btus* (Abhidharmasamuccaya, p. 6) explains decorum as follows:

> What is decorum? It is to avoid what is objectionable in the eyes of others and has the function of doing just that.

It is an avoidance of evil action from making others the norm.

The difference between self-respect and decorum is that, despite their similarity in avoiding evil actions, when the chance of doing evil actions is close at hand, self-respect means to refrain from evil actions in view of the consideration, "This is no part of mine." Decorum means to refrain from evil action by having made others the norm in view of the consideration, "It is not appropriate to do so because others will despise me." ⟨19a⟩ The primary realm of restraint is the fear that one's guru and teacher and other people deserving respect would be annoyed.

The statement that the function of self-respect and decorum is the basis for refraining from evil action properly emphasizes the necessity of these two in refraining from evil action by body, speech and mind, because if self-respect and decorum are not there, one is incapable of restraining any evil action. If there is no fear about the result that might come from one's own action and no fear that the guru, teacher, and others deserving respect would be annoyed, there is no chance that evil behavior will ever stop.

Non-attachment [*ma chags-pa*]

The *mngon-pa kun-btus* (Abhidharmasamuccaya, p. 6) explains non-attachment as follows:

> What is non-attachment? It is not to be attached to a mode of life and all that is involved with it. It functions in providing the basis for not being caught up in evil action.

It is an awareness in which there is no discontentment and no attachment.

Non-hatred [*zhe-sdang med-pa*]

The *mngon-pa kun-btus* (Abhidharmasamuccaya, p. 6) explains non-hatred as follows:

> What is non-hatred? It is the absence of the intention to torment sentient beings, to quarrel with frustrating situations, and to inflict suffering on those who are the cause of frustration. It functions in providing a basis of not getting involved with evil behavior.

It is an awareness in which there is no intention to inflict suffering since, in view of any one of the three possibilities by which I can become an object of hatred, the rise of hatred has been crushed.

Non-deludedness [*gti-mug med-pa*]

The *mngon-pa kun-btus* (Abhidharmasamuccaya, p. 6) explains non-deludedness as follows:

> What is non-deludedness? ⟨19b⟩ It is a thorough comprehension of (practical) knowledge that comes from maturation, instructions, thinking and understanding, and its function is to provide a basis for not becoming involved in evil behavior.

It is a distinct discriminatory awareness to counteract the deludedness that has its cause in either what one has been born into or what one has acquired.[36]

These three last mentioned mental events—non-attachment, non-hatred, and non-deludedness—are the root of everything positive and the means of ending all evil behavior. They are like the very heart of all paths. Since they are there for getting rid of the three poisons and their tendencies on all levels and paths and for becoming disgusted with each of the three poisons which are the cause of evil action, it has been said that they function as providing a basis for properly refraining from evil forms of behavior.

The divisions (one can make) are infinite, but broadly speaking, all the levels and paths come together in these three.

To understand non-attachment as turning one's mind from this life so as not to be attached to it, but still looking forward to a future life, is the attitude of inferior persons. To turn away from desire in being unattached to all the good things of life is the attitude of a mediocre man. To be non-attached to both *saṃsāra* and *nirvāṇa*, but to look forward to a non-localized *nirvāṇa*, is an attitude of a superior man. To explain it this way is only a hint to those who have an inquiring mind—because

---

[36] See *mkhas-'jug*, fol. 43b–44a.

how is it possible to explain here everything that is necessary? ⟨20a⟩ The same argument applies to non-hatred and non-deludedness.

In this context, non-deludedness is a distinct discriminative awareness. In the above statement about what one has obtained by birth and what one has acquired, the former comes from the maturation of that which one has done in previous life, not by the conditions of this life. Therefore, one speaks of what comes from maturation. What one has acquired is that which comes through listening, thinking, and contemplating.

The basis of what one has to listen to with a discriminative awareness derived from studying are the Buddha's teachings and the commentaries. The teachings have twelve divisions:[37]

1. sūtra
2. geya
3. vyākaraṇa
4. gāthā
5. u(d)dāna
6. nidāna
7. avadāna
8. itivṛittaka
9. jataka
10. vāipulya
11. adbhūtadharma
12. upadeśa

Since a detailed explanation of their specific function and which of these is the most important would take many words, it will be omitted here.

These twelve divisions can be condensed into nine according to the master Candrakīrti. He considers the four up to *nidāna* as one.

The nine again ⟨20b⟩ can be condensed into three groups:

---

[37] For a full explanation, see *Abhidharmasamuccaya*, pp. 78–79.

1. sūtrapiṭaka
2. vinayapiṭaka
3. abhidharmapiṭaka

The main content of these three baskets are the three trainings. The main content of the *sūtrapiṭaka* is the training in mental integration, that of the *vinayapiṭaka* is the training in discipline, and that of the *abhidharmapiṭaka* is the training of one's critical capacity.

Just as it has been said repeatedly, the *mngon-pa kun-btus* (Abhidharmasamuccaya) states that the *sūtrapiṭaka* deals equally with the three trainings, the *vinayapiṭaka* explains both discipline and mental integration, and the training of one's critical cognition is explained by the *abhidharmapiṭaka*. The purpose of this rendering is that when one preserves by proper inspection and knowledge [dran-shes] the basic and subsidiary rules of the *vinaya*, this facet becomes the best means for the growth of *samādhi* (integration) because it has the power to end, once and for all, elation and despondency. Today, there are very few who understand this gradation of the path.

Thus, certainty is produced by striving to hear many times the expositions of the three trainings which are the foundations of what is to be studied, and by investigating, over and over again, the meaning of what has been heard by means of the four methods of critical investigation.[38]

Since it is affirmed by the great charioteers that a thorough experience of the path in its totality is accomplished by thinking about it and by settling on the content of this certainty that has come from thinking about it, it stands to reason that intelligent people ⟨21a⟩ will set out on a path in which the Buddhas delight. But those who give up learning which is the real course of a distinctive discriminating awareness are like sheep following blind fools and idiots. Boasting, without ever having thought, and merely preserving their utter laziness, they think

---

[38] For the four methods of critical investigation, refer to p. 37.

that they now have a noble mind, that they have fulfilled a religious life, and that they have spiritual attainments. They merely waste the unique occasion that they have as human beings. Worse than this are those who hold themselves to be superior even when people in the same situation perish and the (Buddha's) teaching declines. These people had better concern themselves with this discriminative appreciation which we have just discussed above. The *mdo sdud-pa* (Prajñāpāramitā-saṃcayagāthā, fol. 11b) states,

> How will millions of millions of blind men
> Ever enter a city without knowing the road to it?
> Without appreciative discrimination, the other five
>   perfections are blind.
> Therefore, without this appreciative discrimination (the
>   blind man's guide), Enlightenment cannot be attained.
> When one is taken hold of by appreciative discrimination,
> He regains his sight and is called the Enlightened One.

And also, the honorable Maitreya says,

> Any preconceived idea regarding the gift, the giver,
>   and the receiver[39]
> Is considered to be a mental obscuration.
> Any preconceived idea regarding avarice
> Is an emotional obscuration.
>
> Everything but appreciative discrimination must be given up.
> Therefore, discrimination is the highest (value).
> And since its basis is learning,
> Learning is the highest (value). ⟨21b⟩

And Aśvaghoṣa says,

> Knowing little, the blind men do not know how to bring
>   contemplation to life.
> Because they lack that, they cannot think of anything.

---

[39] H. V. Guenther, *Jewel Ornament of Liberation*, p. 110, n. 22.

> Therefore, by bringing contemplation to life by
>   continually thinking about the basis of
> Striving towards learning, appreciative discrimination
>   will increase.

And Vasubandhu says,

> He who is disciplined and possesses learning
> Will practice the way of bringing contemplation to life.

Thus has it been stated over and over again in the Sūtras and commentaries.

Diligence [brtson-'grus]

The *mngon-pa kun-btus* (Abhidharmasamuccaya, p. 6) explains diligence as follows:

> What is diligence? It is the mind intent on being ever active, devoted, unshaken, not turning back and being indefatigable. It perfects and realizes what is conducive to the positive.

The mind ever intent on the wholesome is diligence. Therefore, Vasubandhu says,

> What is diligence? It is the antidote against indolence and is that which makes the mind move out towards the positive.

And the *spyod-'jug* (Bodhicaryāvatāra, VII, 2) states,

> What is diligence? It is the inclination towards the wholesome.

Nowadays, in society, there are those who claim that every endeavor is a case of diligence, but striving for this life here is not diligence. Diligence means going out to the positive, but the attempt to shun what one must do in this life means to cling to evils contrary to diligence. ⟨22a⟩

In classifying diligence, the *byang-chub lam-rim chen-mo* gives three:

1. Diligence which is ever ready
2. Diligence which collects wholesome things
3. Diligence done for the sake of sentient beings

But the *mngon-pa kun-las-btus* (Abhidharmasamuccaya, p. 6) explains five:

1. Diligence which is ever ready
2. Diligence which is applied work
3. Diligence which is not to lose heart
4. Diligence which does not turn back
5. Diligence which is never satisfied

The first is to put on the heavy armor[40] in view of the fact that, before one embarks on positive action, the mind must first be made to go out in that direction. Regarding that, the *phar phyin bsdus-pa* (Pāramitāsamāsanāma) states:

> If one, indefatigably, with a mind bent on the wholesome,
> Is compelled to act properly as regards to oneself and others
> In a manner which is likened to the one-pointedness of mind
> Of the Supreme Enlightenment whose vastness is
>   like the ocean which is
> Made up of infinite numbers of water drops, and
> If determination is of long duration in the manner that a year
> Consists of the coming together of those days and nights
> Of a great expanse in which a day and a night
> Is likened to the termination and equanimity of the
> Endless rounds of birth, then he will attain

---

[40] Heavy armor refers to the armor of strenuousness. The armor [go-cha] has been explained in the *Collected Works of sGam-po-pa* (Nga 5a and Dza 2a) as follows: One must pursue the paths wearing two armors, the external which is the armor of seeing, and the internal which is the armor of discriminative awareness. Also, Klong-chen-pa, in his *Zab mo yang thig* (*sNying thig Ya-bzhi*, Vol. 11, p. 77) speaks of four armors. In putting on the armor of trust, one will endure hardship. In putting on the armor of learning, one will destroy external and internal postulates. In putting on the armor of assiduous striving, one will experience realization. And by putting on the armor of humility, one will not cling to fame.

The Supreme Enlightenment which is ever active.
When the mind, having been released from the frustrations of
One's round of *saṃsāra*, becomes ever active,
Immovable and infinite, that (mind) becomes possessed of
The capacity towards the wholesome which is a brave
    mode of action,
And is said to be the first of the pure things to be grasped.

The second ('diligence which is applied work') ⟨22b⟩ is twofold:

1. Steady engagement
2. Enthusiastic engagement

when by application the mind goes out to make a real experience.

The third ('diligence which does not lose heart') is to develop this outgoing of the mind without weakening it by thinking, "How is this possible by me?" It is just as the *skyes rab* (Jātakamāla) states:

To be released on account of faintheartedness is useless.
Therefore, don't be afflicted by misery
But rely on a knowledgeable person who has gained
    the meaning of the teaching.
Then even the most difficult will be easily attained.

Therefore, one should not be afraid nor be unhappy
To do what is necessary, but as circumstances
    should warrant,
He should be encouraged by the splendor of the Wise
And go out to attain all those (positive) values.

The fourth ('diligence which does not turn back') is to make the mind go to its limit without letting it ever be changed by conditions. Regarding this, the venerable teacher (Tsong-kha-pa) says,

When diligence which does not turn back wears its armor,
The virtue of intuitive understanding increases
    like the crescent moon.

All activities of experiencing the path become
  meaningful, and
Whatever is begun will result in the manner that
  one wishes.

From understanding it thus, the Sons of the Victorious One
Begin with diligence, the big wave which sweeps away
  all indolence.

The fifth ('diligence which is never satisfied') is an effort to seek more than the previous and not to be contented with just a little. Moreover, to take a small portion of the path as the most important one ⟨23a⟩ and to reject all others is a great hindrance to implanting the inclinations regarding the path in total; therefore, it is very important to have a clear understanding of the entire path. The *lam-rim chen-mo* states:

Ārya Asaṅga had stated over and over again that even if one knows properly the way of how to strive after the wide and great, it is very important to have two qualities: 1. one must not despair, and 2. one must not be satisfied with merely some triviality. To think that a great portion of the path is established if only one aspect of it arises, whether it be an apparent quality or the real quality, and to be content with attending to it habitually, even though it has been taken from the teachings and represents logical forms to those who know the essence of the path—this may be acceptable as part of virtue. But to understand that one cannot proceed anywhere by that alone, to leave despair behind, to seek indefatigably the specific positive value of a higher level with a total commitment, and to learn whatever one must learn without ever failing in one's efforts—this is indeed a wonderful thing.

That this activity is said to function as the realization and completion of all positive values means that all positive values depend on diligence. Therefore, ⟨23b⟩ the *lhag bsam bskul-ba* (Adhyāśayasaṃcodanasūtra) states:

What is to be done in this world, and
What is to be done in the world beyond,

Is not difficult for one who exerts diligence.
The positive values of the wise result through
    the power of diligence.

Those who have entered the Enlightenment of the Buddha,
Having seen the detriment that comes from indolence and
    sleepiness,
Always make diligence the basis of endeavor.
This I have always told them to do.

And the *mdo sde'i rgyan* (Mahāyānasūtrālaṃkara, XVI, 65–66)
states:

Of the positive values, diligence is supreme.
Therefore, he who relies on this truly attains the real.
By diligence, one instantly gains the sublime states
Of the mundane and transcendental.

By diligence one attains the desired mode of life.
By diligence one also becomes transformed.
By diligence one becomes free by standing above
    worldly things.
By diligence the Supreme Enlightenment unfolds completely.

Since all positive qualities come in the wake of diligence, it
is very important to initiate assiduous striving. When one
deeply studies and knows the works that have been mentioned
before, there are very effective means of initiating diligence.
For people with low intelligence like myself, it is difficult to
understand these things merely by dealing with these works.
Although Tsong-kha-pa has stated in his *lam-rim*,

It is very important to know the way to end idleness which is
not conducive to diligence in view of the profit that comes from
making a beginning of assiduous striving and the disaster that
comes ⟨24a⟩ from not doing it. It is important to know how to
realize the powers of 1. active implementation of devoted interest, 2. active implementation of steadfastness, 3. active
implementation of joy, and 4. active implementation of rejection.

Since I cannot put down everything in writing here, one can learn them by looking up the *Bodhicaryāvatāra* and the *lam-rim chen-mo.*

Alertness [*shin-sbyangs*]

The *mngon-pa kun-btus* (Abhidharmasamuccaya, p. 6) explains alertness as follows:

> What is alertness? It is the pliability of body and mind in order to interrupt the continuity of the feeling of sluggishness in body and mind. Its function is to do away with all obscurations.

Alertness is an awareness in which the mind is made to serve the positive as a docile servant serves his master. It interrupts the continuity of the feeling of sluggishness in body and mind.

Alertness is twofold:

1. Physical alertness
2. Mental alertness

Physical alertness means that when through the power of concentration the sluggishness of the body, which does not allow one to do anything, has been overcome, one feels light like cotton floating in the air and the body can be made to work towards any positive value one wishes. Mental alertness means that when through the power of concentration, mental sluggishness has been removed, the mind moves on towards its object without friction and can operate smoothly. It is as the venerable teacher (Tsong-kha-pa) states,

> Concentration[41] is the king that rules the mind.
> When he is seated, he is immovable like Mount Meru. ⟨24b⟩
> If he travels, he goes to all positive values
> And brings about great happiness which consists in the
>   pliability of body and mind.

---

[41] *bsam-gtan,* to let one's intention settle firmly on a certain topic. It is a state in which all discrimination is gone and only integration remains.

The statement here that its function is to do away with all obscurations means that, through the power of alertness, sluggishness of body and mind is cleansed, and, when one has alertness, one is drawn towards integration from within. This integration through its mere spreading increases the feeling of pleasure, and by its mere increase, integration becomes ever more intense, and so one becomes powerful to do away with all obscurations.

Concern [*bag yod*]

The *mngon-pa kun-btus* (Abhidharmasamuccaya, p. 6) explains concern as follows:

> What is concern? From taking its stand on non-attachment, non-hatred, and non-deludedness coupled with diligence, it considers whatever is positive and protects the mind against things which cannot satisfy. Its function is to make complete and to realize all worldly and transworldly excellences.[42]

It is intelligence which realizes the positive and protects the mind from what is unreliable by persevering in diligence and not falling prey to the emotions.

According to the *byang sa* (Bodhisattvabhūmi), there are five kinds:

1. Concern with regard to things in the past
2. Concern with regard to things in the future
3. Concern with regard to things in the present
4. Concern with regard to things which were to be done before
5. Concern with regard to things which continue together with what is done now

---

[42] Worldly and transworldly excellences: the former is related to the physical world, the latter to the way in which a Buddha, an Enlightened One, would see the world.

They have been explained by Tsong-kha-pa as follows:

> To get rid of the evil done in the past by means
>   of the teaching ⟨25a⟩,
> And in the future to think of doing what is positive, and,
>   in the same way,
> In the present to do acts without being absent-minded,
> And to carry oneself in such a way that evil will not rise,
> And to gain control over oneself in thinking that all
>   this is possible,
> Then, in view of the above facets, one acts appropriately.

Since it has been said that its function is to provide a basis for letting the worldly and transworldly excellences all be present, it is very important as the basis of all of the levels and paths. In the same way, Nāgārjuna (Suhṛllekha 13) states,

> The Buddha has stated, "Concern is the basis of immortality,
> Negligence is the state of death." Therefore,
> In order for you to increase the wholesome,
> Always be concerned and be so devotedly.

Equanimity [btang-snyoms]

The *mngon-pa kun-btus* (Abhidharmasamuccaya, p. 6) explains equanimity as follows:

> What is equanimity? It is a mind which abides in the state of non-attachment, non-hatred, and non-deludedness coupled with assiduousness. It is quite dissimilar to a state that gives rise to emotional instability. It is a state where mind remains what it is—a state of being calm and a spontaneous presence of mind. Its function is not to provide occasions for emotional instability.

Equanimity means to make the mind fully concentrated on its objective reference by relying on means and techniques internally ⟨25b⟩ and to generate the nine phases in the process assuring stability of mind gradually.[43] When the nine phases in this process have been completed, one need not seek for counteragents of elation or depression—the mind is there spontaneously as what it is.

In general, equanimity is threefold:

1. Motivational equanimity
2. Feeling equanimity
3. Immeasureable equanimity

---

[43] For the nine phases in the process assuring stability of mind [sems gnas dgu] see *Mahāyānasūtrālaṃkāra*, XIV, 11–14 (P. ed. 108, p. 85, 1.5–2.2):

Because the mind is made to stay with its objective reference,
It cannot wander about to this or that.
Because the mind quickly experiences any distractions,
It returns to its objective reference once more. [11]

The wise one gradually draws
His mind inward, and then,
Because he sees the virtue of this,
He tames his mind through deep contemplation. [12]

He sees distractions as offensive
And subdues unpleasant things on account of that.
When greediness, unhappiness, etc., arise,
He subdues them in the same manner. [13]

Thus, the one who strives assiduously
Will experience the natural state of impermanence directly.
By concentrating intensely on what is present before the mind,
He attains the unconditioned. [14]

These four verses explain the nine phases in the process assuring stability of mind. The nine are:

1. The mind is made to settle on its objective reference ['jug-par byed].
2. It is made to stay with it totally [kun-tu-'jog-par byed].
3. It is made to stay with certainty [nges-par 'jog-par byed].
4. It is made to stay with intensity [nye-bar 'jog-par byed].
5. It is tamed ['dul-bar byed].
6. It is subdued [zhi-bar byed].
7. It is intensely subdued [nye-bar zhi-bar byed].
8. It is made to flow in an integrated manner [rgyud gcig-tu byed].
9. It is made to stay with equanimity [mnyam-par 'jog-par byed].

This statement in the *Mahāyānasūtrālaṃkāra* becomes more lucid when we understand it according to Mi-pham's *gSang 'grel phyogs-bcu'i mun-sel gyi*

The one under consideration here is motivational equanimity.

In the first phase of this stabilizing process, one has to know thoroughly the methods which set the mind on its object and then, how its state with this object deepens after one uses what counteracts elation and depression, how to use these counteragents when this deepening takes place, how in the end one obtains full concentration in integration, and how to obtain this equanimity in between periods when one watches for elation or not. All this one can learn from the *byang-chub lam-gyi rim-pa*.

The statement that equanimity functions as not providing occasions for instability means that when these nine phases of the process assuring stability of mind have been completed, it is easy to turn back the manifest emotions which belong to the world of desires. In particular, when composure sets in, elation or depression do not come about.

Non-violence [*rnam-par mi 'tshe*]

The *mngon-pa kun-btus* (Abhidharmasamuccaya, p. 6) explains non-violence as follows:

> What is non-violence? It is an attitude of loving kindness belonging to non-hatred. Its function is not to be malicious.

Non-violence is patient acceptance which expresses itself in the sentiment of how wonderful it would be if suffering sentient beings could be released from all their frustrations. Patient acceptance is an attitude not marred by the slightest idea of inflicting suffering ⟨26a⟩.

---

spyi-don 'od-gsal snying-po (fol. 59a–61b) where he relates the nine phases to the six powers [stobs-drug] and the four mental controls [yid-byed bzhi] [See Appendix, Figure 2, p. 119]. Mi-pham continues by saying, 'These nine phases are completed through five stages. The first one is like a waterfall over a steep mountain. The second one settles like the water in a pool at the foot of the fall. The third one flows like a river. The fourth one is calm like the depth of the ocean. The fifth one stands firm like a mountain.

This non-violence and the rejection of harming others is the central idea of the Buddha's teaching. It has been explained as follows (in the *vinaya*):

> True patient acceptance—patient acceptance difficult
>   to attain—
> Has been said to be real *nirvāṇa* by the Buddha.
> A monk who harms another and who acts violently
> Towards another is not a religious person.

To fulfill the *vinaya*, it is necessary to carry about a water strainer in order to avoid harming life in water. Since a person who does not carry a water strainer is one who goes against loving kindness taught by the Buddha, he must be uprooted from his foundation of harming another and be earnestly advised of the need to actualize the four attitudes by which one becomes an ascetic, namely,

1. Even if one is reviled, he should not revile in return.
2. Even if one is angered, he should not retaliate with anger.
3. Even if one is struck, he should not strike back.
4. Even if someone pries into one's affair, he should not pry into someone else's affair.

Therefore, when those who have insight truly understand these four attitudes, they will necessarily conclude that the renunciation of violence is the quintessence of the teaching.

In case one should think that this is all there is to these eleven positive factors, one should know that the eleven, beginning with confidence-trust, are said to be wholesome by their very nature in view of the fivefold classification of the positive:

1. Wholesome by its very nature
2. Wholesome by being related
3. Wholesome by being related to that which follows
4. Wholesome by inspiring
5. Wholesome in the ultimate sense

They are spoken of in this way because they originate as the wholesome by just being there, independent of other factors such as causative circumstances. ⟨26b⟩ Therefore, it is in this context that they are explained as the eleven primary positive factors.

That which is known as 'wholesome by being related' are the mind and mental events that are associated to each other by means of the five functional co-relations which operate at the level of the eleven positive factors beginning with confidence-trust.

That which is known as 'wholesome by being related to what follows' are those experientially initiated potentialities of experience which are wholesome.

That which is known as 'wholesome by inspiring' are actions of body, speech and mind that have been initiated through confidence.

That which is known as 'wholesome in the ultimate sense' is called the absolute. One labels this positive because, when one meditates on the absolute, all obscurations are removed—but it is not a concrete positive.[44]

These positive factors that have been explained can be divided according to the occasion in which they occur:

1. Wholesome by being inborn
2. Wholesome by means of involvement
3. Wholesome by what has been done
4. Wholesome by being involved with benefiting
5. Wholesome by leaving out nothing
6. Wholesome by being a counteragent
7. Wholesome by being in a state of rest
8. Wholesome by being similar to the cause

'Wholesome by being inborn', to give an example, is confidence-trust which has been set up by the latent potentialities

---

[44] Absolute is ideal, the ideal is ultimate positive. This is not a concrete positive *judged* as positive.

that have come from a previous life independent of what one does about it in this life.

'Wholesome by means of involvement', for example, is the desire to become a Buddha by relying on the four conditions:

1. To rely on spiritual friends in this life
2. To listen to the teaching of the Buddha
3. To pay proper attention
4. To realize what is conducive to the attainment of *nirvāṇa*

'Wholesome by what has been done', for instance ⟨27a⟩, is to pay one's respect to deserving persons.

'Wholesome by being involved with benefiting', for instance, is an activity through which sentient beings reach maturity by four essentials:

1. Charity
2. Speaking kindly
3. Acting in such a way that others benefit
4. Sharing

'Wholesome by leaving out nothing', for instance, are special bright pure actions that make one attain heaven or the good things in life.

'Wholesome by being a counteragent', for instance, is the wholesome action that has special power of overcoming thoroughly all that is not conducive to the positive and all that has to be given up.

'Wholesome by being in a state of rest', for instance, is the truth of cessation (of frustrations) as indicated by the following verse:

> When one becomes separated from cupidity-attachment
> And has overcome evil actions by positive acts,
> He becomes immediately adorned with the Supreme
> And this is called 'having come to rest'.

'Wholesome by being similar to the cause' means the five higher kinds of insight that come with the attainment of the truth of cessation (of frustrations) and the ten powers (of a Buddha).[45]

There is no foundation for considering the wholesome things as entities.

Unwholesome factors are explained in the same manner as being fivefold:

1. Unwholesome by its very nature
2. Unwholesome by being related
3. Unwholesome by being related to that which follows
4. Unwholesome by inspiring
5. Unwholesome in the ultimate sense

The first is, in general, the basic and proximate factors of (emotional) instability.

The second is the mind and mental events which are simultaneous and on the same level as those (unstable) emotions.

The third are the experientially initiated potentialities of experience which are negative.

The fourth are the activities of body and speech initiated by those (unstable) emotions. ⟨27b⟩

---

[45] The ten powers of the Buddha are the ten kinds of knowledge possessed by a Buddha. The ten are:

1. The power to know correctly what is real and what is not real
2. The power to know the relationship between action and its retribution
3. The power to know correctly the depth and progression of contemplative meditation
4. The power to know correctly the depth of man's mental capacity and his potentiality
5. The power to know correctly the limit of man's intellectual capacity
6. The power to know correctly man's ability, his personality, and his action
7. The power to know correctly which actions land one in which existence
8. The power to recall past events correctly
9. The power to know through divine eyes the time of one's death and the good and evil existences in the future
10. The power to know that when one's emotions are overcome, a future existence will not take place, and to know that others will overcome their emotions

The fifth is all that is summarized by *saṃsāra*. Insofar as these are considered to be the situation of the mortals by those who will become elevated, they are said to be unwholesome in the ultimate sense, but there is nothing to establish that everything in *saṃsāra* is concretely an unwholesome thing.

Accordingly, the need to distinguish these unwholesome factors as to their actual and postulated particularities seems to be very important. These unwholesome factors can be divided according to their circumstances:

1. Unwholesome by being inborn
2. Unwholesome by means of involvement
3. Unwholesome by what has been done
4. Unwholesome by harming
5. Unwholesome by leaving out nothing
6. Unwholesome by things not conducive to good things
7. Unwholesome by being destructive

'Unwholesome by being inborn' is exemplified by the impulse to kill, which comes through tendencies implanted in a previous life. There may be a point in making a distinction between the actual act and intention, but even though young people nowadays do not consider this division between good and evil as something very important, it is stated that when one practices the stages as indicated in the *byang-chub lam-rim* it is very important to make this distinction. Hence, without quibbling about words, ⟨28a⟩ one must turn the mind inward and think about it.

'Unwholesome by means of involvement' is, for instance, evil behavior which comes from associating with evil friends, listening to religious freaks, and indulging in sloppy thinking.

'Unwholesome by what has been done' is, for instance, making bloody sacrifices to idols by following those who have been deceived by evil friends in the belief that harming is a religious activity.

'Unwholesome by harming' is, for instance, to harm sentient beings by body, speech and mind.

'Unwholesome by leaving out nothing' is, for instance, activity which sets out on a course and makes certain that there is nothing left but to bestow only painful results.

'Unwholesome by things not conducive to good things' are, for instance, the evil views that obstruct the birth of a path which does not collapse.

'Unwholesome by being destructive' are, for instance, those evil views that destroy everything conducive to that which is wholesome.

'Indeterminate' also covers the range from what is indeterminate in itself to what is indeterminate by being similar to its cause. Moreover, in the positive and negative, there is that which seems to be positive but is not and that which seems to be negative but is not; however, it would be going too far to put it all down here. If you wish to know it thoroughly, then look them up in the Abhidharma texts.

A dictum:

How foolish is the person who indulges in meaningless
    activities
And fatigues himself like one who sifts the grain from
    the chaff ⟨28b⟩
When he rejects the seven jewels[46] which grant all superior
    things in this life and the next
After he has obtained or met them.

The eye of intelligence which distinguishes the path
    from that which is not
Is blinded by the foul waters of the fools and idiots.

---

[46] The seven jewels are: gold, silver, pearl, crystal, beryl, diamond, and coral.

To claim that one can walk the path and scale the
     spiritual levels by using an artificial staff
That resembles the *dharma* is too ridiculous for words.

Oh friends with intelligence and sustained interest,
If you want to search for the jewel that elevates your
     mind to the two positive qualities,
Then follow Tsong-kha-pa, the supreme Bodhisattva, and
Dive deep into the ocean of the Buddha's words which is
     like a Wish-fulfilling Gem.

These few lines are meant to summarize what has been said so
far.

Six Basic Emotions [rtsa-nyon drug][47]

The basic emotions are those emotionally tainted mental
events, namely,

1. Cupidity-attachment ['dod-chags]
2. Anger [khong-khro]
3. Arrogance [nga-rgyal]
4. Lack of intrinsic awareness [ma-rig-pa]
5. Indecision [the-tshoms]
6. Opinionatedness [lta-ba]

The defining characteristic of emotions in general has been
explained in the *mngon-pa kun-btus* (Abhidharmasamuccaya,
p. 43) as follows:

> Whenever something occurs, the characteristic of being
> restless will be present. When that happens, the existential state
> of the mind will be restless. This is the characteristic of emo-
> tions.

An emotion is an ego-centered attitude which makes the mind
restless when something occurs.

---

[47] See *mkhas-'jug*, fol. 6b; as to their origination, see fol. 49a.

Cupidity-attachment ['dod-chags]

Taking each emotion individually, the *mngon-pa kun-btus* (Abhidharmasamuccaya, p. 7) explains cupidity-attachment as follows:

> What is cupidity-attachment? It is the hankering after things ranging over the three levels of existence,[48] and its function is to produce frustrations.

Cupidity-attachment is a mental event which is obsessed with anything by seeing it as being pleasant from its own point of view.

Here, the all knowing master (Tsong-kha-pa) says, ⟨29a⟩

> Cupidity-attachment is a hankering after any pleasurable external or internal object by taking it as pleasing to oneself. For example, just as it is difficult to remove oil stain from a cotton cloth, in the same way, this hankering after and getting more and more involved with the thing makes it very difficult to get rid of.

Cupidity-attachment is threefold:

1. Cupidity-attachment on the sensuous level
2. Cupidity-attachment on the aesthetic level
3. Cupidity-attachment on the non-formulated level

The *mngon-pa mdzod* (Abhidharmakoṣa) explains it as attachment to sensuousness and attachment to possible existences and speaks about the latter by combining the two higher levels into one.

Cupidity-attachment on the sensuous level is sustained interest in and attachment to the five desirable qualities such as color-form, sound, etc.

The combination of the two higher levels into one and calling it 'attachment to possible existence' is for the sake of

---

[48] The three levels of existence are the world of desire, the world of form, and the world of no forms.

removing the error that the experiences taking place on the level of aesthetic forms and on the level of formlessness are the path to liberation.

The statement, 'its function is to produce frustrations' means that, since the foundation of all frustrations of *saṃsāra* on the three levels of existence is the whole process of being reborn into *saṃsāra*, the chief cause of the process of *saṃsāra* is nothing more than the desire for cupidity-attachment. ⟨29b⟩

Anger [khong-khro]

The *mngon-pa kun-btus* (Abhidharmasamuccaya, p. 7) explains anger as follows:

> What is anger? It is a vindictive attitude towards sentient beings, towards frustration, and towards that which gives rise to one's frustrations. Its function is to serve as a basis for fault-finding and for never finding even a moment of happiness.

Anger is a vindictive attitude which is unable to accept the three situations that may give rise to anger and which inflicts suffering on the three situations.

The three situations of anger are sentient beings, one's personal frustrations, and the situation from which these frustrations come.

The reason for saying that the foundation of a vindictive attitude is ninefold is in accordance with the *rin-chen 'phreng-ba* (Ratnamala) which says,

> The vindictive mind comes from nine causes
> Which are vindictiveness towards one's self,
> One's friends, and one's enemy in the three
> Aspects of time[49] and other unfounded fears.

Here the *lam-rim* states,

---

[49] The three aspects of time are, the present, the future, and the past.

Anger is to feel vindictive about sentient beings, frustration, and such things that annoy one such as weapons and thorns. It is a fierce mind which is intent on getting even with all of this.

Anger does not allow one to settle on the pleasures of this life and produces immeasurable frustrations in the next life. Thus, the *spyod-'jug* (Bodhicaryāvatāra, VI, 3–5) states, ⟨30a⟩

> When one is mentally feverish with hate,
> The mind cannot experience peace.
> In not being able to gain either happiness or joy
> One will lose sleep and become very unsteady.

> He who with whatever wealth or honor
> Does kindness will become steadfast.
> They are the assailants who slay
> That tyrant ruler, hatred.

> By anger friends are made weary, and even if one attracts
> Them by gifts, they cannot be made to stay.
> In short, anger does not offer one
> The slightest chance to be happy.

The *skyes-rabs* (Jātakamālā) states,

> If one's face is distorted by the fire of anger,
> Even ornaments will not make it look beautiful.
> Even if one goes to sleep on a comfortable bed,
> The mind burning with anger will be miserable.

> He forgets what good was done for him,
> And being afflicted by anger he goes evil ways.
> He fails in fame and achievements
> And even his prosperity dwindles like the waning moon.

> Even if he is supported by friends, the angry person
> Will fall into ways not suited to being a human.
> While only thinking about "How can I get something" or
>   "How can I harm someone," his intelligence collapses and,
> Generally, he violates the moral norm and becomes more and
>   more infatuated.

When through anger he has become accustomed to do evil acts,
He will for one hundred years suffer evil forms of life.
Even an enemy who is after the evil-doer
Could not be worse than this! ⟨30b⟩

Arrogance [nga-rgyal]

The *mngon-pa kun-btus* (Abhidharmasamuccaya, p. 7)
explains arrogance as follows:

> What is arrogance? It is an inflated mind as to what is per-
> ishable and its function is to serve as the basis for disrespect
> and frustrations.

Arrogance is a mental event which is a kind of inflated mind
making whatever is suitable, such as wealth or learning, to be
the foundation of pride. Here the *lam-rim* states,

> Arrogance bases itself on a nihilistic outlook and gets inflated
> about the high and low, the good and evil of the within and
> without, and assumes superiority.

The statement 'bases itself on a nihilistic outlook' is used because all forms of arrogance come simultaneously with the
belief in oneself and an over-evaluation of oneself.

Arrogance is sevenfold:

1. Arrogance [nga-rgyal]
2. Excessive arrogance [lhag-pa'i nga-rgyal]
3. Pride of excessive arrogance [nga rgyal las kyang
   nga-rgyal]
4. Egoism [nga'o synam-pa'i nga-rgyal]
5. Arrogance of showing off [mngon-pa'i nga-rgyal]
6. Arrogance of thinking small [cung-zad snyam-pa'i
   nga-rgyal]
7. Perverted arrogance [log-pa'i nga-rgyal]

The first is an inflated mind in which one thinks, "Look
here, I am so superior compared to those low creatures."

Excessive arrogance is an inflated mind in which one thinks, "I am better than my peers."

Pride of excessive arrogance is an inflated mind in which one thinks, "I am more exalted than the other exalted ones."

Egoism is an inflated mind in which one thinks, "I am all of what makes up my existence."

Arrogance of showing off ⟨31a⟩ is an inflated mind in which one thinks, "I have achievements," even when one has attained nothing.

Arrogance of thinking small is an inflated mind in which one thinks, "I am so small and inferior compared to those who are so exalted and so high."[50]

Perverted arrogance is to think that it is a virtue to make mistakes like someone who is so proud about his achievements when he is carried away by a goblin. It is just as the *'dul-ba lung* (Vinayāgamōttaraviśeṣāgamapraśnavṛtti) states,

> To feel proud about what is actually a matter of shame is like feeling pride about what one has done to householders and goblins in one's attachment to honor and riches after one has failed and discarded all disciplinary rules.

While this exposition is according to the *mngon-pa mdzod* (Abhidharmakoṣa), the *rin-chen 'phreng-ba* (Ratnamala) classifies arrogance as follows:

> Arrogance is of seven kinds.
> I shall explain them by distinguishing them.
> Regarding them, the person who boasts openly
> That he is equal to or greater than his equal
> From having made the low low and
> The equal either equal or lower,
> Ought to be known as having arrogance of sameness.

---

[50] The implication here is the idea, "The master no doubt is great! I could never reach his height, but look how important I am that I have such a great master!"

> He who is vile, yet venerates himself and
> Boasts that he is particularly great
> Thinking that he is truly ambitious by being lofty,
> Has the pride of excessive arrogance.
> He who boasts about those five meaningless things
> Called 'constituents of the personality',[51]
> Which are vicious like the coming into existence
> Of pus pots, the sprouts of *karma*,
> Is called an 'egoist'.
> When in fact he has not attained anything but thinks that
> He has attained something, he is openly arrogant.
> Praising the performance of evil actions is,
> By the wise, ⟨31b⟩ understood as perverted arrogance.
> To say, "I am useless,"
> Is to belittle oneself.
> This is known as arrogance of self-abasement.
> This is to put it concisely.

Arrogance is the cause for being born into evil existence in a later life and, even when one is born in a human existence, it is the cause for being born in a low caste and as a servant. Through disrespect to those who have (virtuous) qualities, one spoils the opportunity of receiving instructions and understanding them. Thus, arrogance creates unpleasantness both here and in the hereafter. The *rin-chen 'phreng-ba* (Ratnamala) states,

> Inflatedness leads to an evil status,
> Jealousy leads to pale complexion,
> Anger to evil looks, and
> Lack of consultation with learned persons to stupidity—
> The result among human beings is,
> First of all, a hellish way of life.

The *lam-rim* states,

---

[51] These are the same as the five psycho-physical constituents but organized internally as the individual personality.

Since arrogance in this life is the greatest hindrance in the development of one's potentialities[52] and in the next life is the cause for becoming a servant, it has to be given up.

Lack of intrinsic awareness [*ma-rig-pa*]

The *mngon-pa kun-btus* (Abhidharmasamuccaya, p. 7) explains the lack of intrinsic awareness as follows:

What is lack of intrinsic awareness? It is a lack of being aware to one's fullest capacity and it covers the three realms of life. Its function is to serve as a basis for mistaken stubbornness, doubt and emotionality about the entities of reality.

This unknowing is a mental event that is confused about reality as-it-is.

This lack of intrinsic awareness is a confusedness and a pervertedness. Regarding this state of confusedness, the Ācarya Vasubandhu, in his *phung-po lnga'i rab-byed* (Pañcaskandhaprakaraṇa), is of the same opinion as and agrees with the statement of his brother, Asaṅga, in the *kun-btus* (Abhidharmasamuccaya). ⟨32a⟩ Dharmakīrtī, however, talks about pervertedness. Although lack of intrinsic awareness consists of two aspects—confusedness and pervertedness—all authors agree that the main counteragent is discriminative awareness which understands the fact that nothing has an abiding principle.

Lack of intrinsic awareness is twofold:

1. Confusedness about the relationship between one's action and its result
2. Confusedness about the ultimate

The former accumulates actions that will lead to rebirth in evil

---

[52] *lam* (path) is the development of one's potentiality and therefore is not a link joining two points.

existences, and the latter accumulates actions that make us continue in happy existence.

The statement that its function is to serve as the basis for mistaken stubbornness, doubt and emotionality means that, on the basis of unknowing, all other emotions come into existence. On this basis actions are produced, and on the basis of these actions the misery and frustration of *saṃsāra* come about, so that all of the emotions and all evil depends on the lack of intrinsic awareness. So also, it is said in the *rnam 'grel* (Pramāṇavartikā),

> He who sees a self is
> Constantly attached to this ego.
> Through this attachment, he craves for happiness and
> This craving conceals all defects.

And,

> All evils derive from ⟨32b⟩ nihilistic views.
> This is unknowing and from that comes cupidity-attachment.
> And from that, anger and all the rest arise. By that alone
> The cause of evil is explained as 'deludedness'.

And,

> Every instance of evil clings to the root of that (unknowing).
> It is also a view concerned only with what cannot last.

The reverend teacher (Tsong-kha-pa) says,

> The root of whatever one may gain in this world
> Is unknowing. Having seen this, and (then)
> Reversing the order is
> Said to be dependent origination (*pratītyasamutpāda*).

In brief, lack of intrinsic awareness is mentioned as the first member of the twelvefold chain of interdependent origination because it is the root of wandering about in *saṃsāra* and the foundation of all actions and emotions.

Indecision [*the-tshoms*]

The *mngon-pa kun-btus* (Abhidharmasamuccaya, p. 7) explains indecision as follows:

> What is indecision? It is to be in two minds about the truth, and its function is to serve as a basis for not becoming involved with positive things.

Indecision is the mental event in which one oscillates between two extremes concerning the four truths and the relationship between one's action and its result.

This indecision creates obstacles for everything positive and in particular for the vision of the truth. But if one sees the truth, indecision is overcome and one speaks of applying oneself to getting rid of those preconceptions which can be removed by seeing the truth.

Opinionatedness [*lta-ba*]

Emotionally tainted opinionatedness is fivefold:

1. Opinionatedness regarding the perishable constituents ['jig-lta]
2. Opinionatedness regarding extremes [mthar-lta]
3. Clinging to ideologies [lta-ba mchog 'dzin]
4. Clinging to ideologies regarding ethical behavior and compulsive performance [tshul-khrims dang zhugs-mchog 'dzin]
5. Wrong opinion [log-lta]

The first, 'opinionatedness about what is perishable', is explained in the *mngon-pa kun-btus* (Abhidharmasamuccaya, p. 7) as follows:

> What is opinionatedness about what is perishable? ⟨33a⟩ It is any acceptance, claim, opinion as dogma, fiction and opinion about the five psycho-physical constituents as a (eternal) self or

as belonging to a self, and its function is to serve as a basis for all other views.

It is an emotionally tainted appreciation which is concerned with the five psycho-physical constituents as an 'I' or 'mine'.

Such terms as 'acceptance' and so on in the *kun-btus* (Abhidharmasamuccaya) are understood as follows:

Acceptance insofar as one is not afraid of what is contrary to every evidence;

Claim insofar as one is involved with objects which are contrary to all evidence;

Opinion as dogma insofar as one has rationalized it;

Fiction insofar as one is enamored with it;

Opinion insofar as one makes it the content of one's thinking.

The reason for speaking about this view as 'opinionatedness about what is perishable', is as the *lam-rim* states,

> Here, a thing which is perishable is impermanent, and accumulation means plurality. Since the basis of looking and thereby seeing the perishable as perishable is just transitoriness and plurality, one gives it the name of 'view of perishable' because of the statement that there is no eternal and single abiding principle to which a thing may be reduced.[53]

That the function of opinionatedness is to serve as the basis for all bad views is also stated in the *gzhon nu ma bdun gyi rtogs brjod* (Saptakumaryavadāna):

> Where and when will a person ever
> Become detached from the necessities of life and
> Tear out opinionatedness regarding the perishable constituents
> Which is the mother of all biases? ⟨33b⟩

---

[53] The meaning of this passage is that there is no ontological principle or essence which by definition is that by which something is what it is. The assumption of an essence contradicts the axiom of transitoriness.

When opinionatedness regarding the perishable is classified according to its content, there are twenty biases. It becomes twenty by subdividing each of the five constituents by way of four alternatives such as taking color-form as the self, taking the self as having color-form, taking color-form as one's possession, or letting the self reside in color-form and then repeating the same procedure for feeling-tones, ideation, motivation, and perception. Thus it is stated (by Nāgārjuna) in *bshes-sbring* (Suhṛllekha, 49):

> Color-form is not the self.
> Self is not possessed of color-form and color-form
>   is not existing in the self.
> Nor is the self residing in color-form.
> In the same way, the other basic elements
> Ought to be understood as nothing in themselves.

The *bdu-ma la 'jug* (Madhyamakāvatāra, VI, 144–145) states,

> Color-form is not the self, the self does not possess
>   color-form,
> The self does not exist in color-form, nor does color-form
>   exist in the self.
> In the same manner, all four of the basic elements
>   ought to be known.
> They are considered to be the twenty biases
>   regarding the self.
> The vajra-staff which knows that the self—that mountain
>   of biases—does not exist
> Cuts right through and that (imagined) self is instantly
>   destroyed.
> Opinionatedness regarding the perishable constituents
>   dwells on Mount Sumeru and
> Has become its lofty summit.

These twenty kinds of opinionatedness regarding the perishable constituents are explained concisely as the two attachments in the form of 'I' and 'mine', but if you wish to know their concrete nature in detail, this can be learned from the explanation in the *Madhyamakāvatāra*, the *dgongs-pa rab gsal*, and the *Abhidharmasamuccaya* together with its commentary.

The *mngon-pa kun-btus* (Abhidharmasamuccaya, p. 7) explains opinionatedness regarding the extremes as follows:

> What is opinionatedness regarding the extremes? ⟨34a⟩ It is any acceptance, claim, opinion as dogma, fiction and opinion which is completely biased taking the five original elements as eternal existence or as non-existence, and its function is to prevent gaining certainty through the understanding of reality as it comes through the middle way.

It is an emotionally toned appreciation of the self as it is conceived by a nihilistic view ['jig-lta] in terms of absolute eternalism or absolute nihilism.

The *lam-rim* explains these two latter views as follows:

> The opinion holding to an extreme is an emotionally toned appreciation that sees the self, as conceived by the nihilistic view ['jig-lta] as being absolutely eternal or absolutely nihilistic since there will be no subsequent existence.

Therefore, since these bad views make a person fall into the extremes of eternal existence or eternal non-existence, they are the primary obstacles for seeing the middle path which has nothing to do with eternalism or nihilism.

The *mngon-pa kun-btus* (Abhidharmasamuccaya, p. 7) explains clinging to ideologies as follows:

> What is clinging to ideologies? It is any acceptance, claim, opinion as dogma, fiction and opinion to hold the five psychophysical constituents—as far as they are occasions of an opinion about them—as the supreme, the principle, the particularly sublime, and the absolutely real. Its function is to serve as the basis for becoming even more enmeshed in wrong views.

Clinging to ideologies is an emotionally tainted appreciation which overevaluates other wrong views and the constituents of the personality. ⟨34b⟩

The terms such as 'supreme' are here understood as follows:

Supreme is the thought, "How wonderful things are!"

Principle means there is nothing over and above this.

Absolutely real means to hold something as superior and to claim that there is nothing like it.

The *lam-rim* states,

> The opinionatedness of clinging to ideologies is an emotionally tainted appreciation that is concerned with the constituents of the personality of the viewer as they are seen in any one of the three opinions—opinionatedness regarding the perishable, the extremes, and wrong opinion. Thus, opinionatedness is also the cult of what is seen in the light of the ideology.

Its function, which is to serve as the basis for becoming even more entwined in wrong views, means that clinging to ideologies prepares the tendencies of not getting away from evil views in the here and hereafter.

Clinging to ideologies concerning ethical behavior and compulsive performance is explained in the *mngon-pa kun-btus* (Abhidharmasamuccaya, p. 7) as follows:

> What is clinging to ideologies concerning ethical behavior and compulsive performance? It is any acceptance, claim, opinion as dogma, fiction and opinion which holds the five basic constituents and the foundation of ethical behavior and compulsive performance as pure, capable of deliverance from the emotions, and certain to liberate. Its function is to serve as the basis for uselessness.

It is an emotionally tainted appreciation that sees as pure and free a code of behavior that is conditioned by bad views—for example, compulsive behavior ⟨35a⟩ such as wearing certain apparel, adopting mannerisms of speech, and whatever comes out of these things.

The *lam-rim* states,

> Clinging to the ideologies of ethical behavior and compulsive
> performance is an emotionally toned appreciation which is
> opinionated regarding washing away sins, deliverance from the
> emotions, and certainty of becoming disgusted with *saṃsāra* by
> following ethical behavior which renounces morality, compul-
> sive observation which insists on formalities, and modes of be-
> havior and mannerisms of speech and whatever may result from
> them.

The statement that its function is to serve as the basis of use-
lessness is self-explanatory.

The *mngon-pa kun-btus* (Abhidharmasamuccaya, p. 7) explains 'wrong opinion' as follows:

> What is wrong opinion? It is the denial of cause and effect and
> of action and its result, and it negates and does away with what
> is. Wrong opinion is an acceptance, claim, opinion as dogma,
> fiction, and opinion which holds on to error. Its function is to
> eradicate the good, to cut off the root of what is positive, to
> make the root of evil healthy, and to get into evil but not into
> the positive.

It is an emotionally tainted appreciation which sees the relationship of cause and effect of one's action and (the relationship) of earlier and later life as non-existent. Regarding this, the
lam-rim states,

> A perverted opinion is an emotionally toned appreciation
> which denies causation as to a former and later life, the rela-
> tionship between one's action and its effect, and holds that *Śiva*
> or *prakṛti*[54] are the causes of sentient beings. ⟨35b⟩

---

[54] *Śiva* refers to one of the Hinduistic Gods who has been stated here as
an example of a creator God. In the Sāṃkhya system, *prakṛti* is the creative
matter which is believed to be the source of both physical and mental events
that make up the world.

There are four kinds of wrong opinions:

1. Denial of cause
2. Denial of effect
3. Denial of agent
4. Denial of what is in front of one's eyes

Denial of cause is to see good actions, bad actions, etc. as non-existent.

Denial of effect is to see the positive and negative as having no consequence.

Denial of agent is to see father and mother, previous and later worlds as non-existent.

Denial of what is in front of one's eyes is to see the attainments of the Buddhas and Arhats as non-existent.

Although, generally, there are many wrong views, the wrong views that deny the relationship between action and its results and (the relationship) between previous and later worlds are the worst of all because they eliminate everything positive.

Now, if the five kinds of opinionatedness are summarized, they fall under affirmation and negation. Their internal differentiation are: 1. the twenty ways of opinionatedness regarding the perishable; 2. sixty-two bad views; and 3. fourteen indeterminate ones. The sixty-two bad views have been explained in the *mdo sde tshangs-pa'i dra-ba* (Brahmajalasūtra). To list them all individually would go too far, so they are not put down here.

The fourteen indeterminate views are the four views that hold on to the extreme of the past, the four which hold on to the extreme of the future, the four which deal with *nirvāṇa*, and two views which deal with the body and life force. ⟨36a⟩

The four that hold on to the extreme of the past are the views that the self and the world are permanent, impermanent, both, and neither.

The four which hold on to the extremes of the future are the views that the self and the world are eternal, not eternal, both, and neither.

The four which deal with *nirvāṇa* are the views that a Tathāgata will appear, will not appear, will both appear and not appear, and will neither appear nor not appear at the time of (one's) death.

The two which deal with the body and life force are the views that the body and life force are either one substance or different ones.

These views are claimed by the Sāṃkhya [grangs-can], the Cārvāka [rgyang-'phen], the Nirgrantha [gcer-bu-pa], and the Vātsīputrīya [gnas-ma-bu], but in this commentary, only the names of these schools will be mentioned; if you wish to know in detail their individual features and the way in which their distinctions are applied, you will have to study the very precious Sūtras and the Madhyamika works which comment on them.

These views are called 'indeterminate' not because they do not offer anything positive or negative and hence indeterminate, but because the Sāṃkhya philosophers and others start with the premise that the individual personality has an unchanging eternal substance. When one questions whether the self and the world are permanent or not and so on, ⟨36b⟩ they claim that "a system which does not explain the eternal self is unsuitable" and become very upset, instead of explaining the existence of an eternal substance which they claim must be the special foundation if there is to be a particular thing. It is in reply to their view that I say their claim is indifferent (ie., misses the mark).[55]

Thus, the *rin-chen 'phreng-ba* (Ratnamala) states,

> When asked, "Is the world infinite or not?"
> It is said that the Buddha did not answer.
> Why did he not explain such a profound teaching
> To those who do not understand?
> By that (silence) alone, the wise know that
> He is the Omniscient—Knower of everything.

---

[55] See also, Mi-pham's commentary to the *Suhṛllekha*, fol. 52.

The Twenty Proximate Factors of Instability [nye-nyon nyi shu]⁵⁶

The twenty proximate factors of instability are:

1. Indignation [khro-ba]
2. Resentment [khon du 'dzin-pa]
3. Slyness-concealment ['chab-pa]
4. Spite ['tshig-pa]
5. Jealousy [phrag-dog]
6. Avarice [ser-sna]
7. Deceit [sgyu]
8. Dishonesty [gYo]
9. Mental inflation [rgyags-pa]
10. Malice [rnam-par 'tshe-ba]
11. Shamelessness [ngo-tsha med-pa]
12. Lack of sense of propriety [khrel med-pa]
13. Gloominess [rmugs-pa]
14. Ebullience [rgod-pa]
15. Lack of trust [ma-dad-pa]
16. Laziness [le-lo]
17. Unconcern [bag-med]
18. Forgetfulness [brjed ngas-pa]
19. Inattentiveness [shes-pa bzhin ma yin]
20. Desultoriness [rnam-pa gYeng-ba]

Indignation [khro-ba]

The *mngon-pa kun-btus* (Abhidharmasamuccaya, p. 8) explains indignation as follows:

> What is indignation? It is a vindictive intention which is associated with anger when the chance to hurt is near at hand. Its function is to become the basis of taking hold of a knife, killing, and preparing to strike.

---

⁵⁶ See *mkhas-'jug*, fol. 6b.

It is a vindictive intention which intends to strike ⟨37a⟩ when any one of the nine chances for a vindictive attitude is near at hand.

The nine chances for a vindictive attitude are the three ideas of, "he has harmed me, he is harming me, he is going to harm me"; the three ideas of, "he has harmed my relatives, is harming them, and is going to harm them"; and the three ideas of, "he is siding with my enemies, has sided with them, and will side with them." These nine are called the basis of harm according to the previous explanation of their causes.

In case one wonders what the difference is between anger in view of being a basic emotion [khong-khro] and indignation in view of being a proximate emotion [khro-ba], the answer is that anger is a vindictive mind when the above three ideas come before one's mind [dmigs-yul], but indignation is an increase in anger when the chance for harming is at hand and is a very turbid state of mind leading to actual physical harm.

In explaining anger, the *kun-btus* (Abhidharmasamuccaya) says that it is a vindictive attitude concerning the above three ideas and explains indignation as 'the opportunity to harm' and 'taking hold of a weapon'. The *phung-po lnga'i rab-byed* (Pañcaskandhaprakaraṇa) on the other hand explains anger as 'vindictiveness towards living beings', but explains indignation as the immediate act of harming. ⟨37b⟩ If this is what the two brothers, Asaṅga and Vasubandhu, have to say, intelligent people should study the problem deeply since it is very difficult to understand. The function of indignation as harming others offers no problems.

Resentment [khon du 'dzin-pa]

The *mngon-pa kun-btus* (Abhidharmasamuccaya p. 8) explains resentment as follows:

> What is resentment? It is not letting go of an obsession which develops through association with the anger which underlies it. Its function is to be the basis of non-endurance.

It is an intention in which one will not let go of the continuous feeling of resentment and in which one retaliates measure for measure. Its function, not to tolerate, is easily understood.

Regarding these two mental events, the *rin-chen 'phreng-ba* (Ratnamala) states,

> Indignation is an unsettling event in the mind,
> And resentment comes in its wake.

Slyness-concealment [*'chab-pa*]

The *mngon-pa kun-btus* (Abhidharmasamuccaya, p. 8) explains slyness-concealment as follows:

> What is slyness-concealment? It is to perpetuate a state of unresolvedness [kha-na-ma-tho-ba] because of its association with dullness and stubbornness [gti-mug] when one is urged towards something positive. Slyness-concealment has the function of preventing one from making a clean break with it and feeling relieved.

It is the intention to cover up one's evil through stubbornness when one's spiritual friends or others, in their desire to help one, raise the point of one's evil. ⟨38a⟩

By concealing one's evil and not admitting it, evil, however small, will grow bigger and bigger and will provide a cause for not allowing one to make a clean break with it and feel relieved. It will throw one into evil forms of existence later on.

Spite [*'tshig-pa*]

The *mngon-pa kun-btus* (Abhidharmasamuccaya, p. 8) explains spite as follows:

> What is spite? It is a vindictive attitude preceded by indignation and resentment forming part of anger, and its function is to become the basis for harsh and strong words, to increase what is not meritorious, and not to allow one to feel happy.

It is the urge to use harsh words of disagreement due to anger and resentment when others raise one's shortcomings, because one has no intention to make a clean break with evil and get it out of one's system.

Concerning this, the *phung-po lnga'i rab byed* (Pañca-skandhaprakaraṇa) explains 'revile by harsh words' to mean 'to ridicule'. But the *mdzod 'grel* (Abhidharmakoṣavyākhyā) explains that spite originates from believing vice to be virtuous and from overevaluating ideas. By these one plunges into many evil actions such as speaking harsh words. Many non-meritorious situations are generated so that in this life one cannot feel happy and, in the next one, unpleasant results are brought about.

Jealousy [phrag-dog]

The *mngon-pa kun-btus* (Abhidharmasamuccaya, p. 8) explains jealousy as follows:

> What is jealousy? It is a highly perturbed state of mind ⟨38b⟩ associated with aversion-hatred which is unable to bear other's excellences by being overly attached to gain and honor. Its function is to make the mind unhappy and not to allow one to feel happy.

It is a highly perturbed mind which is unable to bear excellences of others because of its attachment to wealth and honor.

This brings about, both here and in the next world, great unpleasantness. In this life there is unhappiness, and, in the next one, one will be thrown into evil forms of existences.

Avarice [ser-sna]

The *mngon-pa kun-btus* (Abhidharmasamuccaya, p. 8) explains avarice as follows:

> What is avarice? It is an over-concern with the material things in life stemming from over-attachment to wealth and

honor, and it belongs to passion-lust. Avarice functions as the basis for not letting up in one's concern for the material things of life.

Avarice is the state of mind which, by being overly attached to wealth and honor, holds the material things of life to be all that count and is unable to give them up.

In this and the next life, it brings about much unpleasantness. The *zla-ba sgron-me* (Chandrapradīpasūtra) states,

> If fools are attached to this body
> Which is rotting away, or to life
> Which is shaky and has no power of its own
> And therefore resembles more a dream or apparition,
>
> They do many inappropriate things
> And come under the power of evil.
> They are carried out on the carriage of the Lord of Death
> And wander about in hell.

And the *sgo mtha'-yas-pa sgrub-pa'i gzungs* says,

> Sentient beings who get into a fight
> Hold to the basis of their quarrel.
> Should they overcome whatever attachment to the cause
>   they have and
> Get rid of their attachment, they would become powerful.

And there are many more such statements.

Deceit [*sgyu*]

The *mngon-pa kun-btus* (Abhidharmasamuccaya, p. 8) explains deceit as follows:

> What is deceit? ⟨39a⟩ It is a display of what is not a real quality and is associated with both passion-lust and bewilderment-erring by being overly attached to wealth and honor. Its function is to provide a basis for a perverse life-style.

Through the power of being overly attached to wealth and

honor, deceit makes one pretend to be a virtuous person. For example, a hypocrite, although his mind is not at all under control and trained, gives the appearance of being quiet and well-trained, with the intention of deceiving others.

Here, the *phung-po lnga'i rab byed* (Pañcaskandhaprakaraṇa) explains deceit as the display of what is false, and the *lam-rim* explains it in the same manner. The statement that it is the basis for a perverse life style means that there is no other or better way to lead a perverse life than to pretend.

There are five perverse life styles [log 'tsho nga]:

1. Hypocrisy [tshul-'chos]
2. Flattering [kha-gsag]
3. Overpraising [gshogs-slong]
4. Evaluating by possessions [thob kyis 'zal]
5. Seeking wealth by wealth [rnyed-pas rnyed 'tshol]

Hypocrisy means, as stated above, that while one has no (virtuous) qualities, one pretends to have them and puts up an outward appearance so that others will not see through him.

Flattering means to talk smoothly by using words agreeable to the opinions of others for the sake of wealth and honor.

Overpraising is, in the desire for someone else's property, first to flatter him and then to praise what he owns.

Evaluating by possessions means that one puts down another by saying he is so greedy in order to gain something.

Seeking wealth by wealth means that by having become completely obsessed with wealth, one brags about what one has attained previously in front of others by saying, "I was blessed ⟨39b⟩ in such and such a way by this great person."

In brief, going from house to house for alms because one is attached to wealth is not in keeping with what is explained in the teaching, and this is said to be a perverted life. If you do not want to lead a perverted life, then cast away the opinions of others and, in solitude, preserve the rules of discipline without fooling yourself.

Dishonesty [gYo]

The *mngon-pa kun-btus* (Abhidharmasamuccaya, p. 8) explains dishonesty as follows:

> What is dishonesty? In one's desire for wealth and honor, one makes evil good by associating with both passion-lust and bewilderment-erring. It provides an obstacle for getting good counsel.

It is the intent to conceal one's shortcomings from others because one is so attached to wealth and honor.

Nowadays, people like us try to keep our mistakes a secret, but when others find out our hidden secret, we become meek and prudent; ultimately we deceive ourselves.

One should think about this matter over and over again as stated in the *spyod-'jug* (Bodhicaryāvatāra, V, 31–32),

> I am constantly living
> Under the watchful eyes of
> The Buddhas and Bodhisattvas
> Who have unlimited vision.

> Thinking in this way, I should consider
> Self-respect, devotion, and apprehensiveness.

These two, deceit and dishonesty, hinder the obtaining of good counsel in this life and in the next one, and they set up various forms of unpleasantness such as ⟨40a⟩ not meeting spiritual teachers in the Mahāyāna. Therefore, these two are counted among the four bleak things[57] referred to in the Kaśyapaparivarta (Chapter 3).

---

[57] The *Kaśyapaparivarta* lists the following four bleak things [nag chos bzhi]:

1. To lie to one's teacher, guru, or monk
2. To produce regret in the minds of others who have no regret
3. To speak words which neither praise nor glorify nor explicate those who truly seek the Mahāyāna path
4. To praise others with dishonesty and deceit and without a pure feeling

Mental inflation [*rgyas-pa*]

The *mngon-pa kun-btus* (Abhidharmasamuccaya, p. 9) explains mental inflation as follows:

> What is mental inflation? It is joy and rapture associated with passion-lust because one sees as excellences the prospect of a long life and other fragile good things by trusting one's youth and good health. Its function is to provide a basis for all basic and proximate emotions.

It is an inflated mind which is full of joy and rapture in view of health, abundance of pleasure, etc. It is the root of unconcern by generating all other emotions. The *lhag bsam bskul-ba* (Adhyāśayasaṃcodanasūtra) states,

> An inflated mind is the root of unconcern.
> Never treat a poor bhikṣu with contempt
> Or you may not find salvation in an aeon.
> This is the orderly procedure in this teaching.

The *bshes-sbring* (Suhṛllekha, 12) states,

> Look at the vain glory of your social status and appearance,
> Your learning, your youth, and your power as your enemies.

Malice [*rnam-par 'tshe-ba*]

The *mngon-pa kun-btus* (Abhidharmasamuccaya, p. 9) explains malice as follows:

> What is malice? It belongs to the emotion anger, lacks loving kindness, pity, and affection, and has the function of treating others abusively.

It is the desire to treat others abusively ⟨40b⟩ without having kind feelings towards living beings.

Here the various synonyms beginning with lack of loving kindness are explained according to the commentaries which say that 'lack of loving kindness' is one's own inclination to treat others abusively. 'Lack of pity' is the inclination to induce others to treat others abusively. 'Lack of affection' is to be pleased when one hears or sees others acting in such a way.

Its function is easily understood.

Shamelessness [ngo-tsha med-pa]

The *mngon-pa kun-btus* (Abhidharmasamuccaya p. 8) explains shamelessness as follows:

> What is shamelessness? It is not restraining oneself by taking one's perversions as one's norm. It is an emotional event associated with passion-lust, aversion-hatred, and bewilderment-erring. It aids all basic and proximate emotions.

It is a strong subjective tendency [blo] not to restrain one's shortcomings by taking oneself or an ideology as the norm. For instance, when a bhikṣu is in a situation where he might have to consume alcohol and he refrains from doing so by thinking, "It is not for me to do," he takes himself as the norm and this restraint from evil is self-respect. The opposite is shamelessness.

Lack of sense of propriety [khrel med-pa]

The *mngon-pa kun-btus* (Abhidharmasamuccaya, p. 9) explains the lack of sense of propriety as follows:

> What is lack of sense of propriety? It is not restraining oneself by taking others as the norm. It is an emotional event associated with passion-lust, aversion-hatred, and bewilderment-erring. It aids the basic emotions and the proximate emotions.

It is a subjective tendency not to curb (restrain) evil ⟨41a⟩ by taking others as the norm. Again, concerning this, when one is tempted to do evil (and restrains from doing so) and thinks, "It is not proper to be frowned upon by others who are worthy of respect, such as teachers and the Gods who look into the mind of others"—one thus avoids evil by taking others as the norm.

This is decorum. The opposite of this is the lack of the sense of propriety. The *rin-chen 'phreng-ba* (Ratnamala) states,

> Shamelessness and lack of a sense of propriety
> Means not to exercise restraint in view of oneself and others.

The *byang-sa* (Bodhisattvabhūmi) states,

> Self-respect is a Bodhisattva's self-restraint in the knowledge that any indulgences in impropriety is not his way. Decorum is this restraint in fear and respect of others.

Both the lack of self-respect and the lack of the sense of propriety aid all of the emotions and are the causes of all evil. If one does not want to refrain from evil, one cannot protect oneself against it. Therefore, both the earlier and later Abhidharma works state that the lack of self-respect and the lack of propriety are said to be on the same level as and correspond to all unhealthy attitudes. Although more could be said, this will suffice.

Gloominess [rmugs-pa]

The *mngon-pa kun-btus* (Abhidharmasamuccaya, p. 9) explains gloominess as follows:

> What is gloominess? It is the way in which the mind cannot function properly and is associated with listlessness [gti-mug]. Its function is to aid all basic and proximate emotions.

It is a very subjective tendency in which physical and mental ⟨41b⟩ heaviness and sluggishness dominate.

Concerning this, the *rin-chen 'phreng-ba* (Ratnamala) states,

> Gloominess is any lack of activity
> Due to heaviness of body and mind.

The *mdzod-'grel* (Abhidharmakoṣavyākhyā) states,

What is gloominess? It is heaviness of body and heaviness of mind. It is a state of physical inertness and mental inalertness.

The *lam-rim* explains it in the same manner.

The statement that its function is to aid all of the basic and proximate emotions means that all of the emotions increase in intensity on account of gloominess. Therefore, the *lhag-bsam bskul-ba* (Adhyāśayasaṃcodānasūtra) states,

> Whoever rejoices in sleep and sluggishness
> Will have a distorted view of his world,
> As when body fluids, air and bilious fluids
> Become excessively present in the body.
>
> Whoever rejoices in sluggishness and sleep will be dulled
> Just as food which has turned bad is not healthy.
> When the body is heavy, the complexion will be unhealthy,
> And even one's speech will become incoherent.

And,

> Whoever rejoices in sluggishness and sleep
> Will be dull and take no interest in the *dharma*
> And will shy away from all virtuous qualities.
> And since brightness leaves his life, he will remain
>   in darkness.

Ebullience [*rgod-pa*]

The *mngon-pa kun-btus* (Abhidharmasamuccaya, p. 9) explains ebullience as follows:

> What is ebullience? It is restlessness of mind which is associated with passion-lust that gets involved with ⟨42a⟩ things considered to be enjoyable. Its function is to obstruct quietness.

It is a very subjective tendency which becomes involved with craving and running after what has previously been seen as pleasurable experience. Regarding this, the *rin-chen 'phreng-ba* (Ratnamala) states,

Ebullience is an utter restlessness in body and mind.

The *phung-po lnga'i rab byed* (Pañcaskandhaprakaraṇa, P. ed. 113, p. 238, 4.3) says,

> What is ebullience? It is the unsettled mind.

The *lam-rim* elaborates this by stating,

> Its objective reference is a pleasant and enjoyable object. Its observable quality is a restlessness of mind and a move towards its object. And since passion-lust predominates, ebullience proceeds in the observable quality of craving. Its function is to hinder the mind from settling on its reference.

It is not proper to think that every instance of the mind going out towards something is a case of ebullience. This ebullience is a preponderance of cupidity-attachment and there are many instances when the mind goes out towards its object by way of other emotions which are not passion-lust. Since a mind can go out towards its objective reference without there being any emotions involved, every going out towards its object is not a case of ebullience.

Lack of trust [*ma dad-pa*]

The *mngon-pa kun-btus* (Abhidharmasamuccaya, p. 9) explains the lack of trust as follows:

> What is lack of trust? It is the mind associated with the category bewilderment-erring which does not have deep conviction ⟨42b⟩, has lack of trust, and has no desire for things positive. It provides the basis for laziness.

It is a preponderance of dullness which is not conducive to trust. There are three kinds:

1. Lack of trust which does not have a deep conviction regarding the relationship between action and its result and is not conducive to trusting confidence

2. Lack of trust which is not clear about the virtues of the
   Three Jewels, finds no joy in their contemplation, and
   is not conducive to lucid confidence
3. Lack of trust which is not concerned with liberation
   —and does not even want it—and is not conducive to
   longing confidence

Its function is easily understood.

Laziness [*le-lo*]

The *mngon-pa kun-btus* (Abhidharmasamuccaya, p. 9) explains laziness as follows:

> What is laziness? It is an unwilling mind, associated with
> bewilderment-erring, relying on the pleasures of drowsiness,
> lying down and not getting up. Its function is to obstruct and
> hinder one in applying himself to positive things.

It is an unwillingness to apply oneself towards the wholesome
since it indulges only in loafing and falling asleep.

Laziness makes all positive things drop away. The *dran-pa
nye-bar bzhag-pa* (Smṛtyupasthāna) states,

> The sole foundation of the emotions
> Is laziness. If, in whatever exists,
> There is found even a trifle of laziness,
> It will be just nothing.

Unconcern [*bag-med*]

The *mngon-pa kun-btus* (Abhidharmasamuccaya, p. 9) explains unconcern as follows:

> What is unconcern? It is to persevere in passion-lust, aver-
> sion-hatred, and bewilderment-erring aggravated by laziness. It
> is not to attend to what is positive ⟨43a⟩ and so also is not to
> protect the mind from those things which cannot provide last-

ing satisfaction. It provides a basis for increasing the unhealthy
state and decreasing healthy ones.

It is a subjective tendency to throw every care to the wind by
not protecting the mind from the emotions and evils which
accrue through them.

The *phung-po lnga'i rab-byed* (Pañcaskandhaprakaraṇa, P.
ed. 113 p. 238, 3.8) states,

> What is unconcern? It is not to attend to what is positive and
> not to protect the mind against the emotions through either
> passion-lust, aversion-hatred, bewilderment-erring, or laziness.

Its function is easily understood.

Forgetfulness [brjed ngas-pa]

The *mngon-pa kun-btus* (Abhidharmasamuccaya, p. 9) explains forgetfulness as follows:

> What is forgetfulness? It is a fleeting inspection which is
> simultaneous with and on the same level as the emotions. It
> functions as the basis of distraction.

It is a flash of awareness in which the mind is not made clear
and forgets immediately the positive thing because it is an
attention to an emotionally tainted object. Thus, since the
phung-po lnga'i rab byed (Pañcaskandhaprakaraṇa) declares
that forgetfulness is an emotionally tainted inspection, to be
oblivious to and dim about a positive mental attitude is said to
be forgetfulness. Since an emotionally tainted object having
pleasant or unpleasant characteristics does not become the
object of the mind, it cannot impress the mind; therefore, this
cannot be called 'forgetfulness'.

Its function of distracting means that, due to any continually tainted inspection, the mind is uneasy concerning the
emotionally tainted object ⟨43b⟩.

Inattentiveness [*shes-bzhin ma-yin*]

The *mngon-pa kun-btus* (Abhidharmasamuccaya, p. 9) explains inattentiveness as follows:

> What is inattentiveness? It is a discriminating awareness which is simultaneous with and on the same level as the emotions and thereby is made inattentive regarding actions by body, speech, and mind. It has the function of providing a basis for falling from one's level of being.

It is an emotionally tainted discriminating awareness which lacks watchfulness with regard to the activities of body, speech, and mind and is not associated with carefulness.

That this inattentiveness becomes the foundation for falling from one's level of being is as the *spyod-'jug* (Bodhicaryāvatāra, V, 26) states,

> A person who is learned and has trust
> But does not apply himself diligently
> Will be sullied by falling from his status
> Because the defect of not being watchful has clung to him.

Desultoriness [*rnam-pa gYeng-ba*]

The *mngon-pa kun-btus* (Abhidharmasamuccaya, p. 9) explains desultoriness as follows:

> What is desultoriness? It is to be a scatter-brain and belongs to the categories of passion-lust, aversion-hatred, and bewilderment-erring. Its function is to obstruct one from becoming free of passion-lust.

It is a mind forced to become distracted from its objective reference through the power of the emotions. The *phung-po lnga'i rab-byed* (Pañcaskandhaprakaraṇa, P. ed. 113, p. 238, 4.2) states,

> The mind is scattered over the five desirable objects of the sensuous world.

If you think that there is no difference between this and ebullience explained above, you should know that 'ebullience' is a going out towards the pleasurableness of an object one has previously known and therefore belongs to passion-lust. Desultoriness is tied up with all three poisons and is concerned with any object and hence these two states are not similar.

There are six kinds of desultoriness ⟨44a⟩:

1. Desultoriness *qua* desultoriness [ngo-bo-nyid gyi gYeng-ba]
2. Desultoriness regarding the without [phyi-rol tu gYeng-ba]
3. Desultoriness regarding the within [nang gyi gYeng-ba]
4. Desultoriness regarding defining characteristics [mtshan-ma'i gYeng-ba]
5. Desultoriness of inappropriate actions [gnas-ngan-len gYeng-ba]
6. Desultoriness by rationalization [yid-la-byed-pa'i gYeng-ba]

Desultoriness qua desultoriness refers to the five sensory perceptions. When one is in the state of meditation, one will rise out of it at any moment when any one of the five sensory perceptions takes place; this is to say that the mind is distracted from its state of concentration.

Desultoriness regarding the without is the going out of the mind towards qualities which do not make one want to stay with them when one has just entered into what is positive through the three activities of listening, thinking, and attending. This is to say that one does not stay with the positive object, but moves towards the opposite.

Desultoriness regarding the within is a craving to relish, a state of elation, depression or indifference in meditation. The reason we speak of internal agitation is that these factors are the main distractions to concentration.

Desultoriness regarding defining characteristics means to apply oneself to the positive when one thinks that he too should do it because others say, "This is meditation."

Desultoriness of inappropriate action is an inflatedness by the idea of 'I' and 'mine' with reference to the feeling of getting into what is positive while depending on the pitfalls provided by (perverted) views, which take what is perishable as the last word about reality, and by arrogance.

Desultoriness by rationalization is like giving up the equanimity of the fourth meditation[58] ⟨44b⟩ for the equanimity of the three lower meditations or to exchange the Mahāyāna for the Hīnayāna.

All of these are called distractions in a general way, but this does not mean that they are all proximate emotions. The first

---

[58] Four levels of meditation [bsam gtan bzhi]: See H. V. Guenther, *Philosophy and Psychology in the Abhidharma*, pp. 216–218; *The Jewel Ornament of Liberation*, p. 89, n. 37. Mi-pham in his *bShes sbring gi mchan 'grel padma dkar-po'i phreng-ba* (fol. 23) states:

The counsel that you must devote yourself to the four levels of meditation means to put into practice intense concentration which will lead you to the excellent state of calm. The first level is threefold in view of it being a counteragent, a benefit, and a state. *Counteragent*: Integrated actions which are in accordance with observation and discursiveness removes emotional instabilities such as the desire to torment and the desire to strive after sensuous objects. *Benefit*: One enjoys the joy and satisfaction which arise from one's solitude. *State*: The concentrated and integrated state of mind. The second level: The mind having been freed of observation and discursiveness experiences only joy and satisfaction. The third level: The mind having been freed of joy which is an indifference to composite things and introspective understanding experiences only satisfaction. The fourth level: The mind having been freed of even the satisfaction of purity and equanimity, has only a feeling tone of equanimity and is integrated concentration. In gaining these four levels of meditation, all frustrations and unhappy states of the mind are overcome.

See also, Klong-chen-pa's *Mkha' 'gro yang thig* in *Snying thig Ya bzhi*, Vol. 5, pp. 184–188.

one is indeterminate and the last one is positive. The real proximate emotion of desultoriness is the desultoriness regarding the without and the within. An intelligent person should study this distinction carefully.

Thus, these twenty proximate emotions from indignation to desultoriness are said to be the proximate factors of instability because they are very close to the basic emotions or associated with them. Moreover, they must also be known individually as to their relationships, for instance, whether the proximate factor of instability, indignation, is close to or associated with the basic emotion anger. Such things are made clear in the Abhidharma texts quoted many times previously. [See Appendix, Figure 3, p. 120.]

The Four Variables [gzhan 'gyur bzhi][59]

The four variables are:

1. Drowsiness [gnyid]
2. Worry ['gyod]
3. Selectiveness [rtog-pa]
4. Discursiveness [dpyod-pa]

Drowsiness [gnyid]

The *mngon-pa kun-btus* (Abhidharmasamuccaya, p. 10) explains drowsiness as follows:

> What is drowsiness? By making the cause of drowsiness its point of departure, the mind is agreeable to the positive, negative, indifferent, timely, untimely, appropriate, and inappropriate. Drowsiness is related to bewilderment-erring. Its func-

---

[59] See *mkhas-'jug*, fol. 8b.

tion is to become the basis of slipping away from what must be done.

It is a strong subjective attitude in which the perceptive organs which operate on the object are made to turn helplessly inward because of being preoccupied with the heaviness of body, little excitement, weariness, and a general haziness. ⟨45a⟩

Here, the statement 'timely and untimely' is elaborated by Nāgārjuna (Suhṛllekha, 38) who says,

> Oh great beings! During the day and even
> During the night, the time after sunrise and sunset,
> Even while asleep, let the time not be fruitless!
> Don't let inspection slip away during those times.

One must understand that the time to sleep is during the night. The time during the forenoon, afternoon and daytime, not being the time to sleep, is the time for striving assiduously to do positive actions.

The statement 'appropriate and inappropriate' is employed for the sake of understanding that during the night sleep is appropriate for increasing the ability of the body to attend to positive tasks; but sleep which is disturbed by the emotions, even if it be during the night, is inappropriate. The reason for this can be known from the texts quoted above.

Its activity is explained as 'slipping away from what must be done' because sleep has two aspects—the positive and negative. The negative aspect of sleep which is emotionally tainted makes one dread positive tasks which must be done. The positive aspect of sleep is explained in detail in the *sa-sde* (Bodhisattvabhūmi), but since it would require too many words to quote it, I shall omit it.[60] ⟨45b⟩

---

[60] The positive aspect of sleep is sleep which is restful and which is without upsetting dreams.

Worry [*'gyod*]

The *mngon-pa kun-btus* (Abhidharmasamuccaya, p. 10) explains worry as follows:

> What is worry? It is an obsession regarding the positive, negative, indifferent, timely, untimely, appropriate and inappropriate on account of anything to be done intentionally or unintentionally and is related to bewilderment-erring. Its function is to obstruct the mind from becoming settled.

Worry is produced from impressing over and over again on the mind what is not pleasing in view of actions made through continually thinking, "Is what is to be done appropriate or not?" or of actions induced through what others may say.

Worry also has the three aspects of being positively toned, negatively toned, and neutrally toned. To worry about offensive things done previously is positively toned. Worry which is produced from having done pleasurable things is negatively toned. To worry little about the situation of work which may profit or may not profit someone else is neutrally toned.

The statement 'timely and untimely, appropriate and inappropriate' means that if one worries in time which still holds a promise, it is appropriate, and if one worries in time which does not hold a promise, it is inappropriate. The appropriateness of worrying in time which still holds a promise is like the necessity of making confession now because, although *karma* has not yet matured, one will have to worry later about the evil. Worry in time which holds no promise is like being born into evil existence from the maturation of man's actions and, since the life of a blind man or a cripple is the situation in which maturity has been completed, it cannot be altered. ⟨46a⟩ Therefore, if one studies deeply the treatise of the *mngon-pa kun-btus* (Abhidharmasamuccaya), it will certainly become the most wonderful occasion for gaining certainty in the gradation of the path.

Selectiveness [*rtog-pa*] *and Discursiveness* [*dpyod-pa*]

The *mngon-pa kun-btus* (Abhidharmasamuccaya, p. 10) explains selectiveness together with discursiveness as follows:

> What is selectiveness? It is a mental addressing that takes in everything in the wake of intention or appreciative discrimination. It is a coarse mental operation. What is discursiveness? It is a mental addressing which is attentive to one thing at a time in the wake of intention or appreciative discrimination. It is an exact mental operation. It has the function of becoming the basis of happiness or unhappiness.

Selectiveness is a rough estimate of the thing under consideration and discursiveness is an exact investigation of it.

The *phung-po lnga'i rab-byed* (Pañcaskandhaprakaraṇa, P. ed. 113, p. 238, 4.3–4.4) says,

> What is selectiveness? It is a mental addressing which ranges over everything. It is a coarse mental operation which is a particular aspect of intention and appreciative discrimination. What is discursiveness? It is a mental addressing which is attentive to one thing at a time and accordingly is an exact mental operation.

The two brothers (Asaṅga and Vasubandhu) seem to agree with this explanation.

The statement, 'it is the basis of happiness and unhappiness', means that since both selectiveness and discursiveness have a positive and negative aspect, the positive aspect of both ought to be known as the basis of happiness because by the positive aspect pleasant results occur; the negative aspect of both ⟨46b⟩ ought to be known as the basis of unhappiness because by the negative aspect unpleasant results occur.

Moreover, selectiveness regarding the significance of 'no abiding substance', in view of getting out of *saṃsāra* and being discursive about it, is the positive aspect. To be selective about pleasant or unpleasant objects, kindled into action by passion-lust, aversion-hatred and so on, and to inspect them in detail, is the negative aspect. Selectiveness and discursiveness regarding situations, behaviors and so on, which are neither positive nor negative with respect to the mind, is the indeterminate aspect.

The reason for calling drowsiness, worry, selectiveness and discursiveness 'the four variables' is that they become positive, negative, or indeterminate according to the level and quality of the mental situation. Generally, the emotionally tainted drowsiness, worry, selectiveness and discursiveness obstruct every aspect of the positive—specifically, the three kinds of higher training.

The five obscurations, stated in the Sūtras, are expressed by Ārya Nāgārjuna (Suhṛllekha, 44) as follows:

> Ebullience, worry, a mind to injure (malice), sluggishness,
> Drowsiness, cupidity-attachment, and doubt—
> Know well that these five are the thieves
> Who rob one's wealth of the positive.

The five obscurations are counted as five because ebullience and worry ⟨47a⟩ are considered as one obscuration; drowsiness and sluggishness are also considered as one; and a mind to injure, cupidity-attachment, and doubt are counted individually.

These five obscurations, such as drowsiness, mean that, in general, all positive (training) and, in particular, the three kinds of higher training, are obscured. Cupidity-attachment and a mind to hurt obscure the higher training in self-discipline. Drowsiness and sluggishness, ebullience and worry obscure mental training. Doubt, selectiveness and discursiveness obscure training in appreciative discrimination.

The *mngon-pa kun-btus* (Abhidharmasamuccaya) says that by these five obscurations, rules of self-discipline and concentration are obscured, but the *sdom-pa nyi-shu-pa'i 'grel pa* (Saṃvaraviṃśakaṭīkā) says that only concentration is obscured. In short, since the explanations in other texts are almost the same as the Abhidharma works, there is no need to explain them here.

Now then, how is it that sluggishness which operates as a proximate factor of instability and drowsiness which operates as a variable are considered as one in the situation of the five obscurations? In the same way, how is it that ebullience which operates as a proximate factor of instability and discursiveness which operates as a variable are considered to be one? Sluggishness and drowsiness are not the same. Sluggishness is a part of bewilderment-erring. Drowsiness can be either positively or negatively toned; hence, sluggishness is said to be a proximate factor of instability and drowsiness is said to be a variable. In the same way, ⟨47b⟩ with regard to ebullience and worry, ebullience is part of passion-lust. Worry can be either positively or negatively toned; hence, ebullience is said to be a proximate factor of instability and worry is said to be a variable. They are considered as one in the scheme of the five obstructions and said to be one insofar as they start from the same cause, are extinguished by the same antidote, and are identical in their function.

That they occur from the same cause means that both sluggishness and drowsiness start from over-stuffing oneself with food, from an unhappy mind, from a fainthearted attitude, and from relishing things. Both ebullience and worry start from indulging in the pleasures of the senses, playing around, laughing, and believing the fiction that one will not die.

That they are extinguished by the same antidote means that both sluggishness and drowsiness are overcome by an awareness of light, and ebullience and worry are overcome by holding the mind to an inner object (idea).

That they agree as to their function means that they agree

because sluggishness and drowsiness make the mind withdraw inward and thus they obstruct concentration. Even worse, they obstruct lucidity of ideas and so they prevent the mind from being completely concentrated.

Thus, for my own edification, I have explained in a small way the basic emotions, the proximate factors of instability, and the four variables. It is very important to know the individual characteristics of the Buddha's teaching: the manner in which *karma* originates from its cause; the way in which the individual objective reference is simultaneous with and on the same level as the specific (emotion); the way in which it becomes a positively toned, negatively toned, or indeterminate attitude by being similar to one or another; the way in which the indeterminate one is indeterminately obscured ⟨48a⟩ or indeterminately unobscured; the way in which each blemish of a stained objective reference is removed by its antidote; the method of rejecting what relates to the worldly path; the particularities of the method of rejecting what belongs to the transworldly path; the particularity of rejecting emotions in insight and in contemplation; the particularity of rejecting emotional afflictions and intellectual afflictions, and so on. But since it is impossible to explain everything here, one should study the pure expositions of the Buddha, which have been explained in the works of the great charioteers who have been predicted by the Buddha, and, particularly, the works of Asaṅga and Nāgārjuna from which I have quoted lavishly, as well as the *legs-bshad* of Tsong-kha-pa, the second Buddha, who has explained them in detail.

A few verses:

> It is certain that emotions are enemies who
> Torture us by hundreds of unbearable pains and agonies,
> Having strongly fettered us by a thousand chains of actions
> In the prison of the world since beginningless time.

And they are also the intolerable thieves who
Whip us so that we do not rest a single moment and who
Steal the slightest happiness and prosperity in
Solitudes and monasteries that are too close to the tempting
   jungle of the world.

Who is more stupid than a man ⟨48b⟩ who takes this
Enemy since beginningless time into his heart as his dear
Friend and who holds as his enemy the sentient beings in
The six worlds who have been one's helpful parents.

Better it is for intelligent and thoughtful persons
To take into their hearts the Wish-fulfilling Gem that
Cherishes and esteems one's helpful parents and
Tears out from their hearts the enemy of the emotions.

A Summary for
Making a Living Experience of
What is Gained by
the Analysis

If one thus knows the structure of the mind and mental events, it becomes important to use this understanding as a means to train oneself. Otherwise, it is of little use, for it only starts arguments with others, makes one talk too much in order to win over someone to one's own side, and makes one strive to pile up synonyms. It is just as the *ting-nga-'dzin rgyal-po* (Samādhirājasūtra) states,

> I have explained the teaching good in every respect, but
> If you, from studying it, do not put it into practice,
> It, like a great medicine for disease held only in one's hand,
> Will not be able to nourish one back to health.

And the *lhag-bsam bskul-ba* (Adhyāśayasaṃcodānasūtra) says,

> The bark of the sugarcane does not have anything.
> The flavor of sweetness is inside. By eating the bark,
> A person will never be able to get
> The sweet flavor of the sugarcane.

> Words are like the bark. To think about
> The meaning is the sugar. Therefore,

> Give up this delight in words and think
> About the meaning by being constantly attentive.

As stated above, when one has become wise in distinguishing what is positive and what is negative, and if one applies oneself with diligence solely to experience the stages of the path, and if one fully understands the basic and proximate emotions as explained above, one can learn to recognize them at once when they arise, by scrutinizing them over and over again ⟨49a⟩ in one's existence, and can immediately overthrow them. As it is said in the *spyod-'jug* (Bodhicaryāvatāra, V, 108),

> The existential state of the body and mind
> Must be examined over and over again.
> This is indeed, in brief, the
> Characteristic of preserving one's awareness.

Ārya Nāgārjuna says (Suhṛllekha, 17),

> Know that the mind is just like a
> Painting on water, sand, or stone.
> Those who have emotions belong to the first,
> The last and the best are those who desire the Dharma.

And from the mouth of dGon-pa-ba,[61]

> With regards to overcoming emotions, one must know their evil, their specific characteristic, their antidotes, and the reason for their origin. From knowing their evil, one must take fault-finding as an enemy, but if one does not know their evil, one will not realize them as an enemy who, as the *mdo-sde'i rgyan* (Mahāyānasūtrālaṃkāra) and the *spyod-'jug* (Bodhicaryāvatāra) state, is the driving force. If with regard to knowing the specific characteristic of the emotions, one does not heed the teaching of the Abhidharma, then, as the *phung-po lnga'i rab-byed* (Pañcaskandhaprakaraṇa)[62] states,

---

[61] dGon-pa-ba is a famous personage belonging to the bKa'-gdam-pa school.

[62] The following passage occurs in neither Candrakīrti's nor Vasubandhu's version of the *Pañcaskandhaprakaraṇa*.

Once one has understood the basic emotions and the proximate factors of instability as they are present in one's existence, the moment attachment or hate arises, he will come to grips with them, as he will be fully aware of what has come up.

Therefore, the moment an emotion arises in us, we must take hold of it by thinking, 'this is it'. Then by investigating the causes and conditions that produced it and the objective reference to which it is related, and by knowing the emotions as evil enemies spying on one's weakness, we must turn it back by its antidote. ⟨49b⟩ The spiritual friend, Phu-chung-ba says,

> Even if I be conquered by the emotions
> I shall escape from under the floor.

As the all-knowing (Tsong-kha-pa) says,

> Emotion is different from any ordinary enemy who, even if he has been vanquished, will come out fighting again after he has regained his strength. Emotion, once it is removed from one's own being, having no place else to go, will not return again. But since we do not strive to remove it, it returns again.

As we do not know which emotion is the basis of this *saṃsāric* existence, and even if we know, since our counteragent of assiduous striving is weak, the emotions recover. But if the counteragents were strengthened, we certainly would be able to overcome them. Just as the all-knowing (Tsong-kha-pa) says,

> When the emotions make their appearance, they should be attentively guarded with inspection from thinking about the evil they can do and the benefits one would gain in being separated from them. Every time an emotion raises its head, throw spears at it over and over again. As soon as any one of the emotions appear in one's life-stream, think of it as an enemy and fight it. Grapple with it so that it will not have a chance to appear. If done improperly, there will be no cure, and there will be nothing you can do about it.

The *spyod-'jug* (Bodhicaryāvatāra, IV, 45–46) states,

An ordinary enemy, even if he is banished from a country
Will remain in some other country and, when he has recovered,
Will return from there increased in strength.
But the way of emotion is different. ⟨50a⟩

Each emotion is destroyed by the eye of discriminating
    awareness.
Once removed from one's mind, where could it go?
Where would it rest to gain strength to harm one?
If I do not strive assiduously due to my weak constitution,
    it will be the end of me.

In brief, the spiritual friend, dGon-pa-ba, says,

What else is there but to watch over one's mind day and night?

And it is said,

When Ye-'bar asked sNu'u-zer, "What are all your spiritual
friends to make the foundation of their counsel tomorrow?" He
replied, "Either the confrontation with direct awareness or
tutelar Gods. Since the cause and result of action increases
progressively, how is one to continue one's vigilance over one's
commitments? Even if one has meditative attainments, one
must see to it that emotions, like the loss of intrinsic awareness
become fewer and fewer and less and less in strength."

In the same manner, at the appropriate times and in between,
to search one's mind and apply antidotes to any emotion that
comes, is the most important, and the very essence of all endeavor, for gaining what is positive in life. Accordingly, the
reliance on spiritual friends must begin from healthy positive
factors such as confidence-trust, and at any moment of one's
endeavor, one must see how these are to be set up properly.
One must by all means make constant effort to apply inspection
and knowledge in order to set up what has not yet been set up
and to let that which has been set up grow ever more.

May we be protected at all times by the Buddha, the fabu-
    lous tree, the only one who brings life to the world
    and its Gods,

Who completely removes worldly afflictions with drops of
    camphor, the three spiritual pursuits, which come from
Buddha's auspicious marks, which grow like flowers
On the wide branches of our practice of the six perfections,
    whose shade grants great joy which is beneficial to
    sentient beings, and
Which blossom ever more radiantly from the trunk
    of the jewelled mind growing from the pure soil
    of renunciation. ⟨50b⟩

The great Bodhisattvas, brilliant and complete, who are
Renowned as the two great ones (Asaṅga and Nāgārjuna)
    among the six ornaments of India,
Took many Wish-fulfilling Gems and the three spiritual
    pursuits
From the store of jewels, the Buddha's teaching—which is

Difficult to understand by those inferior beings
Who are afraid of the deep and wide teaching,
    and difficult to measure.
These Bodhisattvas created waves in the shape of the
    various suggestive and direct meanings
And flooded the glorious country of India with them.

By the compassion of all the Buddhas of all the worlds
The Lord named Matibhadra (Tsong-kha-pa)
Made clear, like the sun, the whole teaching of the
Great charioteers in this northern country.

Those who do wrong actions become the helpers
    of Anaṅga (Cupid),
And become degenerate by the clouds of stupidity
Which are the waves of this degenerate age, and thus
They become inflated by seeing this degeneration as the
    best possible world.

Because I lack fortune, I am born at the end of time,
And, my training being small, my mental eye does not
shine at all.
Therefore, whatever I have not said here or have
said wrongly,
I confess to the wise.

My mental eye has been spoiled by the poison
of impatience,
My heart is torn by the demons of the eight
worldly concerns,[63]
I am not only made contemptible, but even wrathful
by them,
And there is nothing I can do about it. ⟨51a⟩

May I and all beings, through this positive (pursuit),
Be accepted by the true friends of the sublime spiritual
pursuit
And become one who can hold all the teaching
In its width and depth.

May I become like Mañjuśri in setting free
All beings without exception and gain the courage
Of not giving up kindness to others in difficult
Situations which must be examined deeply.

I, Ye-shes rgyal-mtshan, having been urged over and over
again by such religious people as Blo-bzang-bzang-po, the ascetic who explained the Sūtras and Tantras, took up the subject
matter. Having heard a little of the Buddha's teaching from the
venerable, all-knowing, Blo-bzang-ye-shes-dpal-bzang-po, and
having received proper instructions in the *byang-chub lam gyi*

---

[63] The eight worldly concerns [chos brgyad] are: gain and loss, fame and
disgrace, praise and blame, pleasure and pain.

rim-pa from the venerable great spiritual master Blo-bzang-rnam-rgyal and the Lord over all the teaching who goes by the name Maitreyanātha, I composed this work, called 'The Necklace of Clear Understanding: An Elucidation of the Working of Mind and Mental Events' (*sems dang sems-byung gi tshul gsal-bar ston-pa blo-gsal mgul-rgyan*), by making the Abhidharmasamuccaya and its commentary the basis and embellishing it with statements from Tsong-kha-pa and his disciples in the solitude of brka-shis-bsam-gtan-gling temple on the border of Nepal and Tibet.

References

Appendix

Index

APPENDIX

Figure 1: Growth-inhibiting and Growth-aiding Forces

Spiritual integration is the indispensable precondition for man to realize his inherent nature. This chart of the 'Growth-inhibiting and Growth-aiding Forces' which operate in the area of spiritual integration is based on Mi-pham's *gSang-'grel*. See Introduction, p. xxiii.

	Five Obstacles		*Eight Counteragents*
Creating Obstacles to Integration	laziness	←	confidence earnest desire (seriousness) effort cultivation of inner potential
	forgetfulness	←	inspection
Basic Obstacles	depression and ebullience	←	alert awareness
Creating Obstacles to Growth of Integration	not doing anything about either state	←	intent
	overdoing things when either state has subsided	←	equanimity

Figure 2: Six Powers, Nine Phases, and Four Mental Controls

Equanimity means to make the mind fully concentrated on its objective reference. Such contemplation generates nine phases in a process assuring stability of mind. "One who strives assiduously will experience the natural state of impermanence directly. By concentrating intensely on what is present before the mind, he attains the unconditioned."

This chart, based on Mi-pham's *gSang-'grel*, relates the nine phases to six mental powers and four mental controls. See also p. 56, n. 43.

Six Powers [stobs drug]	Nine Phases [sems gnas dgu]	Four Mental Controls [yid byed bzhi]
1. Learning [thos-pa]	1. Mind is made to settle ['jog-par byed]	
2. Thinking	2. Mind is made to settle on the real and actual [yang-dag-par 'jog-par byed]	1. To pull back [bsgrims te 'jug-pa]
3. Inspection-memory [dran-pa]	3. Mind is made to settle wholly [bsdus te 'jog-par byed]	
	4. Mind is made to settle intensely [nye-bar 'jog-par byed]	
4. Attentiveness [she-bzhin]	5. Mind is tamed ['dul-bar byed]	2. To loosen [chad cing 'jug-pa]
	6. Mind is subdued [zhi-bar byed]	
5. Assiduous striving [brtsong-'grus]	7. Mind is subdued intensely [nye-bar zhi-bar byed]	
	8. Its flow is integrated [rgyun gcig-tu byed]	3. To release [chad med-par 'jug-pa]
6. Thorough acquaintance [yongs su dris-pa]	9. It is made to stay integrated [ting-nge-'dzin du byed]	4. To stand effortlessly [rdzol-pa med-pa]

Figure 3: The Basic Emotions and the Proximate Factors of Instability

This chart presents a list of basic emotions which give rise to the proximate factors of instability. Here Ye-shes rgyal-mtshan's *Sems-dang sems-byung* is compared with Mi-pham's *mkhas-'jug*. The three poisons—erring-bewilderment, aversion-hatred and cupidity-attachment—give rise to the lack of intrinsic awareness [ma-rig-pa]. According to Ye-shes rgyal-mtshan, man is a complex phenomenon and there is never only one cause for any situation in which he may find himself. For a complete list of the six basic emotions, see p. 64; for the twenty proximate factors of instability, p. 82.

Basic Emotions	*Proximate Emotions*	
	Ye-shes rgyal-mtshan [*Sems-dang sems-byung*]	*Mi-pham* [*mkhas-'jug*]
Anger [khong-khro]	indignation, resentment spite, malice	indignation, resentment, spite, jealousy, malice
Erring-bewilderment [gti-mug]	slyness-concealment, deceit, dishonesty, shamelessness, lack of sense of propriety, gloominess, lack of trust, laziness, unconcern, desultoriness	slyness-concealment, deceit, dishonesty, shamelessness, lack of sense of propriety, gloominess, lack of trust, laziness, unconcern, desultoriness
Aversion-hatred [zhe-sdang]	jealousy, shamelessness, lack of sense of propriety, unconcern, desultoriness	dishonesty, shamelessness, lack of sense of propriety, laziness, unconcern, desultoriness
Cupidity-attachment ['dod-chags]	avarice, deceit, dishonesty, mental inflation, shamelessness, lack of sense of propriety, ebullience, unconcern, desultoriness	avarice, deceit, dishonesty, mental inflation, shamelessness, lack of sense of propriety, ebullience, laziness, unconcern, desultoriness

INDEX

Book Titles

Abbreviations used in text

(Abhidharmasamuccaya, p. 00) refers to Pralhad Pradhan's edition of the Abhidharmasamuccaya, Visva Bharati, Santiniketan, 1950.

MMK, Mūlamadhyamakakārikā [dbu ma la 'jug]

P. ed. refers to *The Tibetan Tripitaka*, Peking Edition, edited by Dr. Daisetz T. Suzuki. Tokyo-Kyoto: Tibetan Tripitaka Research Institute, 1961.

Secondary sources

Broad, C. D. *The Mind and its Place in Nature*, International Library of Psychology. London: Routledge and Kegan Paul, 1968 (eighth imp.).

sGampopa, *The Jewel Ornament of Liberation* (trans. H. V. Guenther). Berkeley: Shambhala, 1971.

Goodman, S. D. "Situational Patterning: Pratītyasamutpāda", *Crystal Mirror*, Vol. 3, 93–101. Berkeley: Dharma Publishing, 1974.

Guenther, H. V. *Buddhist Philosophy in Theory and Practice*. Baltimore: Pelican, 1972.

Guenther, H. V. "On Spiritual Discipline", *Maitreya*, No. 3, 30f. Berkeley: Shambhala, 1973.

Guenther, H. V. *Philosophy and Psychology in the Abhidharma*. Lucknow: 1957.

Sastri, N. Aiyaswami (Ed.). *Ārya Śālistamba Sūtra*, Adyar Library Series, No. 76. Adyar Library, 1950.

Tibetan sources used in Introduction and Notes

mkhas-'jug [*mkhas-pa'i tshul-la 'jug-pa'i sgo zhes-bya-ba'i bstan-bcos*] by Mi-pham 'jam-dbyangs rnam-rgyal rgya-mtsho.

sgom-phyogs dri-lan by 'Jig-med gling-pa, in *Ngagyur Nyingmai Sungrab Series*, Vol. 37.

bdus dang mtha' rnam-par 'byed-pa'i bstan bcos kyi 'grel-pa 'od zer phreng-ba by Mi-pham 'jam-dbyangs rnam-rgyal rgya-mtsho.

rnam mkhyen shing rta, an autocommentary to *yon-tan rin-po-che'i mdzod* by 'Jig-med gling-pa.

chos-dbyings rin-po-che'i mdzod by Klong-chen rab-'byams-pa.

Khrid-yig [*rDzogs-pa chen-po lod-chen snying-thig gi sngon 'groi khrid-yig kun bzang bla mai zhal lung*] by dPal-sprul O-rgyan 'Jigs-med chos kyi dbang-po.

Zab mo yang thig [*sNying thig Ya-bzhi*] by Klong-chen rab-'byams-pa.

lam-nga rim-gyis bgred tshul dangs bcu'i yon-tan thob tshul bye brag tu bshad-pa by dPal-sprul O-rgyan 'Jigs-med chos kyi dbang-po in *Ngagyur Nyingmai Sungrab Series*, Vol. 41.

bshes-sbring gi mchan grel padma dkar-po'i phreng-ba by Mi-pham 'jam-dbyangs rnam-rgyal rgya-mtsho.

gsang-'grel phyogs-bcu'i mun-sel gyi spyi-don 'od-gsal snying-po by Mi-pham 'jam-dbyangs rnam-rgyal rgya-tsho.

Sources quoted in translation-text

dkon mchog ta la'i gzungs (Ratnōlkānāmadhāraṇi),   41

skyes-rab (Jātakamāla),   50, 67

dgongs-pa rjes-'grel (Sandhinirmocanasūtra),   15

dgongs-pa rab-gsal,   77

sgo mtha'-yas-pa sgrub-pa'i gzungs,   86

mngon-pa kun las btus-pa [*kun btus, mngon-pa kun-btus*] (Abhidharmasamuccaya,   11–14, 19, 22–23, 25, 27–29, 31–32, 35, 37–38, 42–46, 48–49, 53–55, 57, 64–66, 68, 72, 74–75, 77–79, 82–86, 88–96, 99, 101–103, 116

mngon-pa mdzod [*mdzod*] (Abhidharmakoṣa),   6, 9–11, 14, 22, 24, 26–27, 41, 65

Technical Terms

Tibetan

Sanskrit

(Untranslated Sanskrit words appear in Name and Subject Index)

Names and Subjects

(*Numerals in italics indicate primary citation*)